750

MAR 2

D0933609

William Carlos Williams
❧ THE LATER POEMS

William Carlos Williams
THE LATER POEMS

JEROME MAZZARO

CORNELL UNIVERSITY PRESS
ITHACA AND LONDON

811.5

First published 1973 by Cornell University Press.
Published in the United Kingdom by Cornell University Press Ltd.,
2-4 Brook Street, London W1Y 1AA.

Acknowledgment is made to Lawrence Pollinger, Ltd., MacGibbon & Kee, Ltd., and New Directions Publishing Corporation for quotations (reprinted by permission of New Directions Publishing Corporation) from the following works of William Carlos Williams.
AUTOBIOGRAPHY. Copyright 1948, 1949, 1951 by William Carlos Williams.
COLLECTED EARLIER POEMS. Copyright 1938 by William Carlos Williams.
COLLECTED LATER POEMS. Copyright 1944, 1948, 1949/1950, 1963 by William Carlos Williams.
IMAGINATIONS. Copyright © 1970 by Florence H. Williams.
IN THE AMERICAN GRAIN. Copyright 1925 by James Laughlin. Copyright 1933 by William Carlos Williams.
PATERSON. Copyright 1946, 1948, 1949, 1951, © 1958 by William Carlos Williams. Copyright © 1963 by Florence Williams (Book VI).
PICTURES FROM BRUEGHEL AND OTHER POEMS. Copyright 1954, 1955, 1962 by William Carlos Williams.
Quotations from the following works of William Carlos Williams are reprinted by permission of New Directions Publishing Corporation. All rights reserved.
SELECTED ESSAYS. Copyright 1954 by William Carlos Williams.
SELECTED LETTERS. Copyright © 1957 by William Carlos Williams.
A VOYAGE TO PAGANY. Copyright 1928 by The Macauley Company. Copyright 1938, © 1970 by New Directions Publishing Corporation.

International Standard Book Number 0-8014-0753-2
Library of Congress Catalog Card Number 72-11549

Printed in the United States of America by Vail-Ballou Press, Inc.

Librarians: Library of Congress cataloging information appears on the last page of the book.

*For Robert Boyers
and Angus Fletcher*

Preface

꽃   Before his death in 1963, William Carlos Williams had achieved for a circle of younger writers the status of elder statesman. He had been of the generation of Ezra Pound, Robert Frost, T. S. Eliot, Wallace Stevens, and Marianne Moore and, in the years following World War II, had gained a popular and academic reputation that had earlier eluded him. He was generous to young writers and, like Stevens and Moore, frequently contributed to new, small literary magazines. Of all the poets of that generation, he remained the most accessible. By its very inventiveness and responsiveness to technological changes, his work became, in language and form, archetypically American, as he was. He persisted to the very end as a polemicist, an experimenter, a rebel, and, above all, a fine lyricist. So, when I was asked in 1968 to deliver a series of three lectures on contemporary American poets at the University of Parma, I thought of no more proper figure to begin with than this respected Rutherford doctor. What follows began as two lectures from that visit. In this form they were published by *Intrepid* as "Of Love, Abiding Love" (1970). The same year I added what became two more sections. Both evolved from a seminar I conducted on modern American poetry at the State University of New York at Buffalo, and they were subsequently printed in *Modern Poetry Studies*. The seed of the last segment was sown at that time, too, but it took me a while to harvest its yield. All the pieces have been expanded and revised since their delivery and publication, and yet, however much the book may owe to these origins, it was not until all the pieces were rewritten that I began to understand the work's total vision.

William Carlos Williams: The Later Poems is a study of the poetics of William Carlos Williams, concentrating for the most part on the late works: *Paterson*, "Asphodel, That Greeny Flower," and "Pictures from Brueghel." These works are seen as attempts to link the phenomenal world of the older writer with the dreams he had in his youth. To the extent that it traces this connection, the study is also a work of exegesis, in at least two traditional senses. Part of the book is a correlation of texts, some of which are readily accessible, others of which are not, but all of which the poet authorized in a lifetime of composition. Williams repeats himself constantly, exfoliating, revising, and developing his ideas as he goes on. Here dating is important, and I have cited dates wherever necessary. I have had recourse as well to that other aspect of exegesis, interpretation, for I have at times found that the key to a repeated phrase may lie buried in some neglected essay or letter or in a persistent metaphorical relationship that is never made explicit. Moreover, since the line between artistic form and life in Williams' work is so often blurred, I have made use of biographical information where it is needed in my interpretation. The *Autobiography* is not always reliable, and I have tried whenever possible to verify whatever incidents I have taken from it. The study also raises questions of form and its relationship to the individual and to culture. Here its subject has proved fortuitous, for Williams was bothered most of his life by his involvement in these relationships. Thus, the book continues a process I began with *The Poetic Themes of Robert Lowell* and continued in *Transformations in the Renaissance English Lyric*. As those works examined the impact of changing religious beliefs and musical structures on poetic form, this concentrates mainly on the impact of science and the revolution in the visual arts.

When I have cited dates for the poet's work, they are inevitably those of publication as given in Emily Mitchell Wallace's invaluable *A Bibliography of William Carlos Williams* (Middletown, Conn., 1968). I have removed italics from several quotations from *Kora in Hell* and James Johnson Sweeney's *Stuart Davis,* only where whole passages have been in italics and not otherwise. I have provided references for the citations made within the text in a note on the abbreviations used. References for the other quotations are to be found at the back of the book. I have benefited greatly from discussions with Joseph N. Riddel and Sister Bernetta Quinn, and from comments, readings, and suggestions made to me by James Bunn, Allen De Loach, William Heyen, and Murray Schwartz. I wish also to thank Karl Gay and the staff of the Poetry Room of the Lockwood Memorial Library in Buffalo for making available to me many of their holdings. I have been aided as well in the work's completion by a grant from the Research Foundation of the State University of New York.

Versions of Chapters One and Three have appeared as "Of Love Abiding" in *Intrepid,* no. 17; copyright 1970 by Jerome Mazzaro. Chapter Two appeared in earlier form as "Dimensionality in Dr. Williams' *Paterson,*" *Modern Poetry Studies,* I (1970), 98–117; copyright 1970 by Jerome Mazzaro. A version of Chapter Five was published as "The Descent Once More: *Paterson V* and 'Pictures from Brueghel,'" *Modern Poetry Studies,* I (1970), 278–300; copyright 1970 by Jerome Mazzaro.

JEROME MAZZARO

Buffalo, New York

x

Contents

❦

A Note on Abbreviations

꧜   The following abbreviations of book titles are used throughout the text, preceding the page number cited. All books are by William Carlos Williams except as noted.

A	*Autobiography.* New York, 1967.
CEP	*The Collected Earlier Poems.* New York, 1951.
CLP	*The Collected Later Poems.* Rev. ed. New York, 1963.
ELG	"Essay on *Leaves of Grass,*" in *Leaves of Grass One Hundred Years After,* ed. Milton Hindus. Stanford, 1955.
FD	*The Farmers' Daughters.* New York, 1961.
I	*Imaginations.* New York, 1970.
IAG	*In the American Grain.* New York, 1956.
IM	*In the Money.* New York, 1967.
IWWP	*I Wanted to Write a Poem,* ed. Edith Heal. Boston, 1958.
ML	*Many Loves.* New York, 1965.
P	*Paterson.* New York, 1963.
PB	*Pictures from Brueghel.* New York, 1962.

PWCW	Mazzaro, Jerome, ed. *Profile of William Carlos Williams*. Columbus, 1971.
SE	*Selected Essays*. New York, 1954.
SL	*Selected Letters*. New York, 1957.
SP	*Selected Poems*. New York, 1963.
VP	*A Voyage to Pagany*. New York, 1970.
WCW	Miller, J. Hillis, ed. *William Carlos Williams*. Englewood Cliffs, 1966.
WM	*White Mule*. New York, 1967.
YMW	*Yes, Mrs. Williams*. New York, 1959.

William Carlos Williams
❧ THE LATER POEMS

CHAPTER ONE

The Man and the Dream

⚜ For William Carlos Williams the poem has at least two existences. It has a relation with nature which he associates with the myth of Kora and a relation with imagination which he associates with some notion of permanence. These associations permit him to write in *Kora in Hell* (1920) that, like some scientific hypothesis, the poetic creation must be tested against the nature it depicts and thereby undergo a cycle of "descent" and "return," and in "Asphodel, That Greeny Flower" (1954) to assert that "only the imagination is real! / I have declared it / time without end" (PB, 179). Similarly, his Prologue to *Kora* can establish a principle of the harmony of imaginations, and "Yours, O Youth" (1922) assert: "Spurious information is that which is unrelated to the contacts of experience. Out of it literature is NOT made" (SE, 32). The same essay can advise with a neoclassicism approximating Alexander Pope's that one "would do well to study the masters," for "the master is he whom one may approach without prostituting himself. It is because in the master's work all things go back to the ground" (SE, 36). "On

1

Measure—Statement for Cid Corman" (1954) can even advocate the reading of Pope: "So, I understand, the young men of my generation are going back to Pope. Let them. They want to be read at least with some understanding of what they are saying and Pope is at least understandable; a good master" (SE, 338).

These discrete natural and imaginative existences of a poem which extend to all of Williams' work permit him to alter his critical attitudes, often with the slyness of a Yankee farmer and always at others' expense, to justify first one position and then its opposite. The practice has enlisted not only his own attacks on T. S. Eliot and Ezra Pound for being "false masters," evidences of his own pique at their exalted reputations, but critical stances with respect to his own work that he eventually refutes. Moreover, these vacillations in positions have drawn Yvor Winters' dismissal of him in a 1965 "Postscript" as an "anti-intellectual," who "did not know what the intellect was." Winters calls him finally a "foolish and ignorant man but at moments a fine stylist" (WCW, 69). Still, Williams never claimed to have a preconceived, consistent, doctrinaire approach to poetry, and one suspects that, over the long run, the approach he did claim, which relies upon the givenness of situations, best resembles the gratuitous process described by Randall Jarrell when he accepted the National Book Award in 1961: "Sometimes I read . . . that I'm one of those poets who've never learned to write poetry. This is true: I have never learned. Sometimes a poem comes to me—I do what I can to it when it comes." [1] As Williams' "In Praise of Marriage" (1945) phrases it, "For the poet words come first and the ideas are caught, perhaps, among them. The poet invents his nets and catches the birds and butterflies of philosophy. It does not go the other way." [2] "No ideas but in things" (P, 14), he was to say; the object rather than the ego takes priority.

These vacillations between nature and imagination convey an approach to poetry close to the visions of both the pre-Cartesian philosophers who saw that in knowledge there could be no absolute separation between the realms of sense and intellect and the pragmatist philosophers— John Dewey, William James, and Alfred North Whitehead —whose work Williams celebrates in "Choral: The Pink Church" (1949). To the extent that it is philosophic, his underlying belief in a concinnity of intellect and body approaches closely that which Ernst Cassirer's *The Individual and the Cosmos in Renaissance Philosophy* describes as obtaining in the work of Nicholas of Cusa: "Thus no intellectual function can conceivably exist dissociated from the realm of sensible material. To become effective, the mind requires a body corresponding and 'adequate' to it. For this reason, furthermore, the differentiation and individualization of the act of thought must be in harmony with the organization of the body." [3] Williams' position is contained in *Kora:* "That which is known has value only by virtue of the dark. This cannot be otherwise. A thing known passes out of the mind into the muscles, the will is quit of it, save only when set into vibration by the forces of darkness opposed to it" (I, 74). This "primal" dark is variously the earth, matter, the id, the destructive counterpart of the libido, the sensible, or the effective principle of Renaissance philosophy. As early as *In the American Grain* (1925), Williams is associating it with "the herd." But whereas Cusanus would make the concinnity of body and mind a basis for individualism, since no two people's eyes would have the same vision, Williams' position makes the objectification a basis of continuity: once lodged in the muscle rather than in the mind, the relationship would be beyond the vicissitudes of individual mental distortion.

Yet such a view of a concinnity of mind and body is not, as critics like J. Hillis Miller have tried to make it, a systematic rejection of the whole dualist dispute of Romanticism. Williams' own despair of "tender-minded" philosophers and philosophical poetry should provide assurance enough of his not having approached his poetry in such a way. Like James in *Pragmatism* (1907), he prefers instead to think of theories as *"instruments, not answers to enigmas in which we can rest.* We don't lie back upon them, we move forward, and, on occasion, make nature over again by their aid."[4] As instruments, their formulations turn "away from abstraction and insufficiency, from verbal solutions, from bad *a priori* reasons, from fixed principles, closed systems, and pretended absolutes and origins." They turn "towards concreteness and adequacy, towards facts, towards action and towards power."[5] To harden them finally into a static position, as Miller does, lies beyond Williams' intention, as would a reader's insistence on the completely fluid state which the poet at times associates with pragmatism. Williams seems to concur with Dora Marsden's attack on the pragmatist notion that "truth is what works: what is, is true." Ignoring James's modification that truth must work "in the long run," her "Lingual Psychology" (1916) asserts: "So that everything is true, and the description applies so universally that it is pointless to apply it to anything in particular."[6] Williams' response, "The Great Sex Spiral" (1917), extends her rejec-

4

tion to a definition of truth he intermittently recurs to: Truth is "the intersection of loci, . . . the place where several sense experiences of differing sorts coincide."[7] Moreover, as a letter to Kenneth Burke (1933) explains, he tended to think of abstract thought and science as male and female halves of a complex knowledge that only art could offer: "From knowledge possessed by man springs poetry. From science springs the machine. But from a man partially informed, that is, not yet an artist, springs now science, a detached mass of pseudo-knowledge, now philosophy, frightened acts of half realization. . . . If I could convince myself or have anyone else convince me that I were merely following in the steps of Dewey, I'd vomit and quit—at any time. But for the moment I don't believe it—the poetry is offered not too confidently as proof" (SL, 137–138).

Earlier, in "Heaven's First Law" (1922), rather than associate Williams with any philosophical school, Burke had called him "the master of the glimpse" and written of his Imagist process: "There is the eye, and there is the thing upon which that eye alights; while the relationship existing between the two is a poem" (WCW, 47–48). John Malcolm Brinnin's *William Carlos Williams* (1963) uses the description to propose that out of such a simple process no sophisticated poetics can result: "Unlike the poet whose lifework is clearly segmented in periods, Williams wrote poems in the 1960's, as he had in every other decade of his career, very much like those he wrote in 1914. . . . He did not so much develop a technique as he exploited a general attitude which determinedly avoided the repetitions on which technique is based. . . . Consequently, Williams' technical development was largely a matter of canny dispositions of language within a limitless area; his philosophical development mainly a matter of the representation of ideas elaborating the view of life with which he began. His technique per se remained comparatively static, allowing for intensification and extension but not for complication." [8]

More practically, the dual, natural and imaginative lives of a poem permitted Williams within the "stasis" of his general technique to shift his developing perception from direct observation to an extended, often fortuitous "parallel between contemporaneity and antiquity" and achieve, as Robert Lowell's "William Carlos Williams" (1963) asserts, an idiom that "comes from many sources, from speech and reading, both of various kinds." The blend of these sources, Lowell continues, "which is his own invention, is generous and even exotic" (WCW, 156–157). The generosity lies in a kind of objectivity which Williams' medical background doubtlessly fostered, an ability to present subjectivity with a degree of impersonality by stressing the experience rather than the experiencer. This emphasis leads often to a third-person style, a passive voice, a reduction of decorative metaphor, and a handling of slang, colloquial expressions, and localisms in an impersonal rather than personal way. Words become objects instead of sources of coloration and come out of, rather than restrict, specific situations. Being the result either of a need to speak or of a need for recollection, they are made more vital by the situations which give rise to them. As Williams explains this process in "Yours, O Youth," "Yet the artist is limited to the range of his contact with the objective world. True, in begetting his poem he takes parts from the imagination but it is simply that working among stored memories his mind has drawn parallels, completed progressions, transferred units from one category to another, clipped here, modified there. But it is inconceivable that, no matter how circuitously, contact with an immediate objective world of actual experience has not been rigorously maintained" (SE, 33–34).

This contact of words with the objective world, Williams' *Kora* announces, is sporadic rather than continuous: "The words of the thing twang and twitter to the gentle rocking of a high-laced boot and the silk above that. The trick of the dance [the poem] is in following now the words, *allegro,* now the contrary beat of the glossy leg" (I, 55). Its value, he adds in "Notes in Diary Form" (1927), lies in its vividness, not in its coloration: "The good poetry is where the vividness comes up 'true' like in prose but better. . . . That thing, the vividness which is poetry by itself, makes the poem. There is no need to explain or compare. Make it and it *is* a poem" (SE, 67–68). "To intensely realize identity," he asserts, "makes it [the poem] live" (SE, 72). This vividness, one suspects from Williams' essay on Marianne Moore (1925), comes when one imitates her practice of "wiping soiled words or cutting them clean out, removing the aureoles that have been pasted about them or taking them bodily from greasy contexts" so that the word stands "crystal clear with no attachments; not even an aroma" (SE, 128). As he explains, "With Miss Moore a word is a word most when it is separated out by science, treated with acid to remove the smudges, washed, dried and placed right side up on a clean surface" (SE, 128). Earlier, *Spring and All* (1923) had insisted that "the word must be put down for itself, not as a symbol of nature but a part, cognizant of the whole—

aware—civilized" (I, 102), and the Introduction to his volume, *The Wedge* (1944), goes on to observe: "There's nothing sentimental about a machine, and: A poem is a small (or large) machine made of words. When I say there's nothing sentimental about a poem I mean that there can be no part, as in any other machine, that is redundant" (CLP, 4). He notes further that "when a man makes a poem, makes it, mind you, he takes words as he finds them interrelated about him and composes them—without distortion which would mar their exact significances—into an intense expression of his perceptions and ardors that they may constitute a revelation in the speech that he uses. It isn't what he says that counts as a work of art, it's what he makes, with such intensity of perception that it lives with an intrinsic movement of its own to verify its authenticity" (CLP, 5).

Williams' Prologue to *Kora* makes this authenticity and lack of sentimentalism a difference between him and other poets: "The true value is that peculiarity which gives an object a character by itself. The associational or sentimental value is the false. Its imposition is due to lack of imagination, to an easy lateral sliding. The attention has been held too rigid on the one plane instead of following a more flexible, jagged resort. . . . Here I clash with Wallace Stevens" (SE, 11). But, as his essay on Marianne Moore points out, the desentimentalization of language must not leave it lifeless ritual: " 'Ritual,' too often to suit my ear, connotes a stereotyped mode of procedure from which pleasure has passed, whereas the poetry to which my attention clings, if it ever knew those conditions, is distinguished only as it leaves them behind" (SE, 127). In *In the American Grain,* he designates the results of the

8

desentimentalization "a ceremonial acknowledgment of the deep sexless urge of life itself" (IAG, 34). Hence, his attempts at a "transcending," desentimentalized language move toward a language which transcends the individual by merging him with the herd into a living tradition. As he was later to tell John C. Thirlwall, "I have defeated myself purposely in almost everything I do because I don't want to be thought an *artist*. I much prefer to be an ordinary person. I never wanted to be separated from my fellow mortals by acting like an artist. I never wanted to be an artist externally—only secretly so as not to be set apart. I wanted to be something rare but not to have it separate me from the crowd" (SL, xvii). Like the truth of pragmatic philosophy, the result of the union never obtains *in saecula saeculorum,* but becomes what works in the long run. Consistent with Sam Adams' fear of a fading and languishing of ideas, quoted by Williams in "The Writers of the American Revolution" (1925), the vitality which keeps its forms relevant tends often in time to diminish. As he told the editors of *A.D. 1952* (1952), "Of course I'm iconoclastic. . . . An artist has to be. A continual break down and build up has to go on. Take the forms in which poems are cast. Most of them are old, not suited to our times. We have to cast about searching for new ones, and when we have found them society will finally accept them and see that other work is cast in those forms. Pretty soon, they will become old hat. Somebody else will have to work to get rid of them." [9]

Thus language, which is the means by which people acknowledge their separation from one another, becomes the means by which they reunite for a time through shared imaginative structures. In his views of this reunion, which links the individual not only with the present but with the past, Williams differs in a second way from Stevens, whose sophisticated view of language and imagination insists that no two imaginations perceive identically and each perception distorts and is distorted by every individual perceiver. At root, Williams maintains his scientific faith in a tradition of writing based upon the assumption that the experience of an experiment can be so written down that it can be repeated by others and verified. Moreover, as he did not create a separate imaginative world devoid of nature, he does not here create a separate inner life, based on potential, which may in time divorce itself from an outer life, based on action. Here, too, he differs from Stevens. For Williams, the inner life must manifest itself in action. Therefore, by recounting action, one recounts the effective inner life. What inner life is not effective (action-producing) is "sentimental." As he relates in his letter to Burke (1933): "Poetry . . . is the flower of action and presents a different kind of knowledge from that of science and philosophy" (SL, 137). Yet, as with scientific language, to achieve this action, words in poetic writing if they should remain vital should receive their "true" (effective, denotative) rather than their "false" (nonproductive, connotative) value.

An understanding of this emphasis on true rather than "sentimental" language allows a reader insight into two other areas. First, it aids him toward an understanding of how Williams' positions as both poet (imaginist) and doctor (scientist) result in the unified existence which his *Autobiography* (1951) avers: "When they ask me, as of late they frequently do, how I have for so many years continued an equal interest in medicine and the poem, I reply that they amount to me to nearly the same thing" (A, 286). The integration of technology and art seems enviable and laudable at a time when the two are so often thought mutually exclusive. "As a writer," he points out, "I have been a physician, and as a physician a writer; and as both writer and physician I have served sixty-eight years of a more or less uneventful existence, not more than half a mile from where I happen to have been born" (A, ii). Elsewhere, writing of the poem *Paterson,* he expresses the belief that the poet's business is "not to talk in vague categories but to write particularly, as a physician works, upon a patient, upon the thing before him, in the particular to discover the universal" (A, 391). Harvey Breit's "Talk with W. C. Williams" (1950) recalls "the too infrequent visits he made to Rutherford, . . . when he would accompany the doctor—in a fading jalopy—on his rounds. The poet would leave his car, usually quite in the middle of discussing a complex idea, to attend an expectant mother; and the doctor would return fifteen minutes later to pick up the idea without the loss of a syllable." [10] "No matter what I was writing," Williams' "Seventy Years Deep" (1954) recalls, "my practice always came first. The town never found me wanting." [11] Burke's obituary, "William Carlos Williams: 1883–1963" (1963), characterizes the outcome: "In essence, this man was an imaginative physician and a nosological poet" (WCW, 51).

Early, "Notes from a Talk on Poetry" (1919) had equated science and poetry with emotion: "Knowledge is a fleeting emotion. Science is an emotion. . . . Poetry is a language of emotion." Already the accomplishments of scientists were being equated with those of Villon, "whose ink was frozen in the pot when he finished writing his

Petit Testament," and Williams was asking, "What is the discovery of radium to Mme. Curie today? . . . what is her discovery to her but a stale, useless thing, a thing she would forget in a minute if she could equal it with another as great? It is to her exactly nothing save the end of the circle, exactly where the beginning was—a serenity, a stasis, a community with her masters. And what is that but an emotion?" [12] Later, "Seventy Years Deep" would add that Rutherford's proximity to New York City afforded medical and literary opportunities that a similar community in Indiana or Minnesota might not: "I attended clinics in New York for years to perfect myself in my specialty, the diseases of children. . . . I could attend a literary gathering most any week night and get home without missing an appointment, and on Sundays I could spend the day exchanging thoughts with the 'promising' intellectuals of the times." [13] Nonetheless, *Spring and All* and *A Voyage to Pagany* (1928) reveal that the management of his dual interests in medicine and literature was not always happy.

Spring and All suggests that most of Williams' life had "been lived in hell—a hell of repression lit by flashes of inspiration, when a poem such as this or that would appear" (I, 116), and, through Doc Evans, the hero of *A Voyage to Pagany,* he expresses the view that his trip to Europe in 1924 was an attempt to "let the whole works go. I should never think of the practice of medicine again. Never!" As Williams explains, "Evans had practiced medicine all his adult life, so far, up to his present fortieth year, in a continuously surly mood at the overbearing necessity for it— wanting always to do something else: to write!" (VP, 4). Only at the end of the journey has Evans learned that literature cannot be divorced from life, from the soil, from

America, and he returns to practice medicine. This knowledge is carried by Williams into "A Novelette" (1929), written during a January influenza epidemic. The doctor-narrator acknowledges that writing provides relaxation and relief; he does it "to have nothing in my head—to freshen my eye by that till I see, smell, know and can reason and be" (I, 229). He says of medicine's contribution to vision: "It is because the stresses of life have sharpened the sight. Life is keener, more pressed for place—as in an epidemic, the extraneous is everything that is not seen in detail. There is no time not to notice" (I, 273). At one point he even admits, "It was damned clever, making a diagnosis like that and saving a baby's life, worth more than any poems, I think" (I, 279). Writing to Robert McAlmon in 1947, he restates his need to write to relieve himself of his tensions and confesses, "I wish I could smash the hell out of where I am—but I've always felt that way and done nothing about it except write, which gives me a kind of escape" (SL, 255). All the same, the two professions were so fused that he could not imagine where he could go after he quit his practice, if he ever did. "Seventy Years Deep" notes: "I loved people. I loved caring for their sick bodies and seeing them get well. The poet's job was similar in a different region, and together the doctor and the poet formed a whole. I found that there were many periods, especially at slack seasons, when one job did not interfere with the other—on the contrary, the alternation actually rested me." [14]

Second, the emphasis on true language explains Williams' aversion to a closed (sentimental) system for imaginative literature wherein poetry and its language exist divorced from life and its language. This aversion, which kept him from hanging his experiences upon the ornamental, abstract bones of plot, major form, or outline, has met with repeated critical resistance. In "John Wheelwright and Dr. Williams" (1939), R. P. Blackmur cites it as reason for a flatness and a lack of culmination: "Dr. Williams has no perceptions of the normal; no perspective, no finality—for these involve, for imaginative expression, both the intellect which he distrusts and the imposed form which he cannot understand." [15] Eleven years before, Pound had outlined Williams' position by stating that when "plot, major form, or outline" are "put on ab exteriore, they probably lead only to dullness, confusion or remplissage or the 'falling between two stools' " (WCW, 35), adding somewhat wryly that Williams "certainly has never loaded on enough shapings to bother one" or to fall (WCW, 35). Even Jarrell's Introduction to the *Selected Poems* (1949) expresses doubts in this area: "Williams' imagist-objectivist background and bias have helped his poems by their emphasis on truthfulness, exactness, concrete 'presentation'; but they have harmed the poems by their underemphasis on organization, logic, narrative, generalization." [16]

Moreover, within this aversion to abstract structure, the poet's efforts to rid language of its false "aureoles" and "smudges" by becoming interested in the cultural context whose particularity gave it its special truth come into clearer focus. In his effort, he joins a wide circle of contemporaries like H. L. Mencken, D. H. Lawrence, Van Wyck Brooks, and Sherwood Anderson, who were trying to chart the peculiarities of the "American" experience. Their efforts go back to Ralph Waldo Emerson's "The American Scholar" (1837) and Walt Whitman's "Democratic Vistas" (1870), wherein distinctions between foreign and American experiences began to be made. In the hands of Mencken, Lawrence, and Anderson, these experiences extended into psychology and language. So, too, with Williams. As Louis L. Martz's "The Unicorn in Paterson" (1960) maintains, *In the American Grain* "seeks a way of moving from an old world into a new; it seeks a way of leaving the finished forms of culture and dealing with the roar, the chaos, of the still-to-be-achieved" (WCW, 78). In its search, the book discerns two modes of thought. One is the Puritan, which represents "the way of all men who lack 'the animate touch,' and who therefore set up within themselves a 're-sistance to the wilderness' which is the new life all about them" (WCW, 78). The vituperativeness here of Williams' position may owe something to Mencken's earlier attacks on Puritanism, although *Poetry* and Harriet Monroe were equally vehement in this regard. In contrast, Williams offers a group of great explorers, "sensitive to the wonder of life all about them in the new world" (WCW, 78).

Yet, however often Williams insisted upon true language and poems springing from situations, a close look at his poems reveals that they are generally constructed upon an unstated, unconscious mythic pattern. They follow a common pattern of mythic descents into hell: Orpheus, who goes down into Hades to rescue Eurydice, or, because of a belief in the perennial and natural equivalents of the descent, Kora, whose descent into the underworld requires a rescue by Demeter. According to depth psychologists, the two patterns of thinking are related and involved with the double. In "Archetypes of the Collective Unconscious," Carl Jung clears up some of the relationship by associating the Orphean descent with the archetype of the "wise old man" or "meaning." Listing guises like those which Williams often assumed in his poems, Jung goes on to explain in "The Phenomenology of the Spirit in Fairytales" that "the Wise Old Man appears in dreams in the guise of a magician, doctor, priest, teacher, professor, grandfather, or any other person possessing authority." [17] Moreover, almost as if he were responding to Williams' repeated statements of writing himself out of periods of despair and spatial closure, Jung moves on to assert, "The old man always appears when the hero is in a hopeless and desperate situation from which only profound reflection or a lucky idea—in other words, a spiritual function or an endopsychic automatism of some kind—can extricate him. But, since for internal and external reasons, the hero cannot accomplish this himself, the knowledge needed to compensate the deficiency comes in the form of a personified thought, i.e., in the shape of this sagacious and helpful old man." [18] In the Orphean form of the myth, it is the same man at two different points of experience, whereas in the Kora-Demeter form, discrete, identical twins stand at either end, representing seed and harvest.

The aim of the wise old man's coming, according to Jung, "is to gather the assets of the whole personality together at the critical moment, when all one's spiritual and physical forces are challenged, and with this united strength to fling open the door of the future." [19] Hence, the persona of the wise old man that the poet assumes at these moments when he is most inundated by duty and harried by work offers not self-mastery but what Jung senses is a "purposeful reflection and concentration of moral and physical forces that comes about spontaneously in the psychic space outside consciousness when conscious thought is not yet—or is no longer—possible." [20] In such a positive, Orphean form, the figure evinces signs of the conscious will's inability alone to reunite the personality to the point where it can acquire the extraordinary power to succeed at its appointed task. Often, as "Seventy Years Deep" reveals, these short poems or short sections of longer poems would come spontaneously: "When the phrasing of a passage suddenly hits me, knowing how quickly such things are lost, I find myself at the side of the road frantically searching in my medical bag for a prescription blank. I practically lose consciousness for the interval it takes me to put the words down. Then, relieved, I continue to the hospital." [21] Often, too, as "Painting in the American Grain" (1954) asserts of painters, the subject matter consisted in "a part of their lives that they had to see re-enacted before them to make it real that they could relive it in memory and re-enjoy it." [22]

Such signs agree with Joseph N. Riddel's contention in "The Wanderer and the Dance" (1970) that Williams' poetry functions at a level of "pre-reflective consciousness," for, in the "dreams" of his poetry, the significance of these or any moments rescued for himself becomes apparent by the mind's making them an automatic substitute for prolonged, self-defining introspection. In this pattern of mythic descents, of rescues from the various constrictions of doctoring and art, *Paterson*, "Asphodel, That Greeny Flower," and "Pictures from Brueghel" (1960) form the most consummate and conscious realizations. As such, they illustrate the final fusion which "The Tortuous Straightness of Charles Henri Ford" (1939) cites as occurring in every man "if he is to be rated high as a master of his art"; the fusion occurs "between his dream which he dreamed when he was young and the phenomenal world of his later years" (SE, 236). The full importance of these poems lies thus not merely in the structures they assume but also in the way, after an interval of nondescending poetry, they relate directly to earlier "descents" like "Sub Terra" (1915) from *Al Que Quiere!* and *Kora* and indirectly or obliquely to such works as "The Descent of Winter" (1928), "The Wanderer" (1914), *In the American Grain,* and *Spring and All.*

Williams' *I Wanted to Write a Poem* (1958) identifies the inspiration of the first as a mood of having been excessively inundated by daily life. The circumstances invite a rescue by Demeter: "I thought of myself as buried under the earth, buried in other words, but as any plant is buried, retaining the power to come again. The poem is Spring, the earth giving birth to a new crop of poets, showing that I thought I would some day take my place among them, telling them that I was coming pretty soon. . . . When I spoke of flowers, I *was* a flower, with all the prerogatives of flowers, especially the right to come alive in the Spring" (IWWP, 21). The same sense of being "buried in other words," of needing some endopsychic automatism to rescue him, motivates the action of *Kora,* where mythical descents and ascents into fall and spring signal the discovery and return of proper language. As Williams explains, "I am indebted to Pound for the title. We had talked about Kora, the Greek parallel to Persephone, the legend of Springtime captured and taken to Hades. I thought of myself as Springtime and I felt I was on my way to Hell (but I didn't go very far)" (IWWP, 29).

The *Autobiography* gets more explicit about the mood prompting the work: "The third book was *Kora in Hell.*

Damn it, the freshness, the newness of a springtime which I had sensed among the others, a reawakening of letters, all that delight which in making a world to match the supremacies of the past could mean was being blotted out by the war. . . . It was Persephone gone to Hades, into hell. Kora was the springtime of the year; my year, my self was being slaughtered" (A, 158). In this cycle, Williams locates art not in the upward thrust but "at the sickening turn toward death." "The pieces are joined into a pretty thing, a bouquet frozen in an ice-cake," he notes in *Kora*. "*This* is art, *mon cher*, a thing to carry up with you on the next turn; a very small thing, inconceivably feathery" (I, 71). In the course of the work, Kora figures are seduced by both Pope Clement (Section VI) and a New Jersey sheriff (Section XVI), and, in Section XV, the poet announces, "All beauty stands upon the edge of the deflowering" (I, 59); and later that "the poet transforms himself into a satyr and goes in pursuit of a white skinned dryad" (I, 60).

During the year that he wrote *Kora*, as a letter to David Ignatow (1948) later states, Williams was having "dreams": "They were wild flights of the imagination. As I look at them now I see how 'romantic' they were. I feel embarrassed. I was having 'dreams' at the time; I was having 'ideas' " (SL, 267). The observation recalls his statement to Burke in 1923: "I suppose I am at heart a mystic. . . . Even the Arabs or the Phoenicians, or whoever it was that invented the rule of three, were mystics until they found out pretty damned clearly that they were fooling themselves and so had to invent the science of mathematics to save their faces" (SL, 54). In his essay on Marianne Moore, he equates this mysticism with vividness and true language:

"Poems have a separate existence which might, if it please, be called mystical, but it is in fact no more than the practicability of design" (SE, 123).

This design, as both *Kora* and *Spring and All* illustrate, was numerical. Besides a series of tensions or pairings of dance and music, male and female, life and art, Europe and America, prose and poetry, reflection and assertion, the works make apparent arrangements in terms of three, the least number on which a pattern may be formed. Both works consist of twenty-seven sections, subdivided into three groups of nine. In *Kora,* random improvisations, like the grace notes of music, violate the work's otherwise strict mathematical code. Nevertheless, a reference to asphodel makes clear that one enters the underworld at the end of Section IX, and a new step toward the other side of the dark identifies one's leaving at the close of Section XVIII. Similarly, the twenty-seven poems of *Spring and All* are interrupted randomly by sections of prose whose concern during the first nine poems is novelty; during the second nine poems, copying and imitation; and during the final nine poems, the differences between poetry and prose. In "The Descent of Winter," Williams begins an investigation into the number four with references to four words engraved in the four corners of an Aztec calendar, making overt the seasonal divisions that had underscored his vision. The number four is repeated in the female love interests of *A Voyage to Pagany* though, like the earlier works, the novel is divided into three sections.

Both Williams' statements and these practices suggest that the poetics of his early poems, crucial for any discussion of his later work, consisted equally of a Romantic belief in poetic vision and a modernist belief in an art work as craft. It is the role of the poet to make his work readable and natural through a kind of "bricklaying" with words, but this, as *Kora* and "The Wanderer" establish, does not preclude the possibility of "dreams" and "ideas." These "dreams" and "ideas" are not, however, glimpses into any Absolute, but, in keeping with the meaning of the "wise old man," prognoses of a future state based upon hope and probability. Williams' "The Basis of Faith in Art" (1937) makes this clear: "We're attempting to track down the origins of a poet's aspirations, what might be called his soul, his longings toward that as yet imaginative new province to which we shall come—tomorrow! That's where our souls are always living" (SE, 186). He seems to have this notion of futurity in mind, too, in 1949 when he writes John Crowe Ransom: "The secret of all writing, all literature, is escape, true enough, but *not* in the Freudian sense. It is not, in other words, evasion. But it *is* escape—from the herd" (SL, 272–273).

Being based upon a future and an escape from the herd, Williams' dreams, as both "The Wanderer" and *In the American Grain* show, by transcending the present condition, do not transcend this world, the very "bricks" of their matrix. His having "dreams," then, becomes no different from any young man's having visions of a better time for himself and the world. As such, they realize perfectly the nontranscendent properties of the "old man" archetype, occurring as it does, when divinity is dead, in the persistence of a continuing, driving daemon of wisdom. In "The Wanderer," Kora's abduction by Pluto under-scores the poet's seizure by a feminine godhead. He is kept until his baptism in the "filthy Passaic," like Kora's eat-ing of pomegranates, makes a complete return to a previous state impossible. This "old woman," he indicates in *I Wanted to Write a Poem,* was his grandmother "raised to heroic proportions." The poem, he notes, was actually a "reconstruction" from memory of his early Keatsian *Endymion* imitation that he thought he had destroyed by burning it in a furnace. It was the story of his growing up: "The old woman in it is my grandmother. . . . I endowed her with magic qualities. She had seized me from my mother as her special possession, adopted me, and her purpose in life was to make me her own. But my mother ended all that with a terrific slap in the puss" (IWWP, 24). "The Three Letters" (1921) treats her in terms more overtly taken from the Demeter-Kora myth. Symbolizing America, she is paradoxically both "a virginal young woman" and one "inclined, of course, to grant important favors to certain individuals of special distinction." [23] In this version, peaches rather than pomegranates are used to seal her pact with the young hero. She returns in "Portrait of a Woman in Bed" (1916), "Dedication for a Plot of Ground" (1917), "The Last Words of My English Grandmother" (1920), and most importantly as the woman with "the Cockney accent" in the closing lines of *Paterson V* (1958).

Something of the same "descent" myth, as it pertains to nontranscendence, obtains in Columbus' discovery of the New World in *In the American Grain.* Williams locates the New World as Hades was located by the ancients, "in those times beyond the sphere of all things known to history" (IAG, 7), and thus makes the voyage metaphorically and unconsciously a parallel to the descent of Kora or Orpheus. Columbus, who is the prototype of all explorers, including poets, by his journey rescues new possibilities. He serves as a vicarious analogue of the "wise old man" at a time when new possibilities could be outwardly and spatially realized. These new possibilities, as Williams' "An Essay on *Leaves of Grass*" (1955) later propounds, since one seemed no longer able to go outside for wisdom, presently extended inward—"into the cell, the atom, the poetic line." He might also have added, "into the mind."

As Riddel's "The Wanderer and the Dance" indicates, the "pre-reflective" self which the persistence of such an archetype confirms is different by its very lack of self-awareness from the conscious rejection of the subject-object dualism that Miller's *Poets of Reality* (1965) designates as the achievement of Williams. Riddel notes that the conclusion of "The Wanderer," which weds the poet to the world and creates his condition of wandering by separating him from the herd, does so by avoiding the method of introspection for self-discovery. The "baptism" or "anointment" into "other" commits him not to a self quest but to a role of participant-observer in which his experiential distinction is quantitative (a single man observing) rather than qualitative (a peculiar consciousness absorbing). In this commitment, the dislocation is similar to a doctor's dislocation in being both subject to human frailty and by knowledge (anointment) able to transcend such failings. The acuteness of this ability to transcend may enter into the qualitative properties of experience by giving its possessor a sense of superiority, and, in Williams' case, there is a never tiring display of this sense in his references to "the herd," in the dogmatic statements that fill his poems, and in his uncanny ability in his works to separate among his acquaintances the sheep from the goats. It is perhaps the archetype of the wise old man subsuming both the doctor and the poet.

Not surprisingly then in the most famous of his early poems, "Danse Russe" (1916), where the narrator is both participant and observer, Williams hits upon the device of a mirror to approximate the double of hero and old man. Earlier, in "The Wanderer" he had asked, "How shall I be a mirror to this modernity?" (CEP, 3). Here the mirror becomes both an image of his poetic field and the means of somatic observation. His dancing naked and grotesquely before it becomes a kind of poem about life's turning into art, indicative of Williams' dual Kora-Demeter role as voyager and rescuer. The poem demonstrates, in addition, his early belief that art should copy nature as well as a typical young man's preoccupation with the present and the future rather than the past. It begins with a movement that expands outward from the speaker's sleeping wife to his household to the world, returning from this accumulative identity to the north room, the mirror, and the image of himself reflected by the mirror against the more restrictive yellow, drawn shades which shut the room off from the outside. He is lonely, "born to be lonely," but equally he is the "happy genius" of his household, the *genius loci*, who rescues meaning out of such loneliness by bringing the world impromptu into order. The rescue is made even more dramatic if one sees the poem as a variation on David's dancing naked before the Ark of the Lord (2 Kings 6:14) and recognizes that God has here become the speaker's mirror image.

Later, as Williams grows older and finds himself relying increasingly upon the dreams of his youth, he associates poetry and its relation to life less with a metaphor of mirror than with memory and the created world of his poem. "The Sound of Waves" (1948) speaks of poetry in terms that recall the origin of Venus, emerging as "a voice! / out of the mist / above the waves and / the sound of waves" (CLP, 172). Yet here, too, as he writes in "Asphodel," "The poem / if it reflects the sea / reflects only / its dance/ upon that profound depth / where / it seems to triumph" (PB, 165). The present can be only one sea surface of the depths which, in a letter to his wife (1927), Williams associates with collective experience: "Another thing I discovered this morning: the sea as I looked at it is exactly the same sea, given the right day and weather, that Columbus, Eric the Red, and the Puritans looked at. Thus it annihilates time and brings us right up beside these men in the imagination. This is a delight to me" (SL, 88).

But most important in the descents of these early works, as Riddel's review of Miller's *William Carlos Williams* asserts, is the matter of language: *"Kora is a language experiment, at times aggressively rhetorical, at others purely impressionistic and verbally subjective. But above all, it is at one and the same time an attempt to destroy language (the language of abstraction) by way of purifying it, and a running commentary on why it must be purified. . . . Kora,* in sum, moves between a subjective and an objective language—is at once experience and explanation of experience." [24] Earlier, Ralph Nash's "The Use of Prose in *Paterson"* (1953) had noted Williams' uses of language, divided by him into prose and poetry, to echo themes. These language experiments, in which the operative mode of a poem becomes its thematic statement, approximate attempts by the poet to devise a style consistent with the mythic patterns of his work, devoid of as much subjectivism as possible, to represent how Williams the desperate, descending hero is also Williams the ascendant, Orphean singer. The mood making the poem is also the poem made. As he explains the process in *Kora*, "That which is heard from the lips of those to whom we are talking in our day's-affairs mingles with what we see in the streets and everywhere about us as it mingles also with our imaginations. By this chemistry is fabricated a language of the day which shifts and reveals its meaning as clouds shift and turn in the sky and sometimes send down rain or snow or hail. . . . But of old poets would translate this hidden language into a kind of replica of the speech of the world with certain distinctions of rhyme and meter to show that it was not really that speech. Nowadays the elements of that language are set down as heard and the imagination of the listener and of the poet are left free to mingle in the dance" (I, 59).

Intimately allied to the problems of language in these early descents and integral to the dreams of youth are the rhythmic units of their manifestations. Speaking of them from the phenomenal world of his later years, Williams says in *I Wanted to Write a Poem*, "The rhythmic unit usually came to me in a lyrical outburst. I wanted it to look that way on the page. I didn't go in for long lines because of my nervous nature. I couldn't. The rhythmic pace was the pace of speech, an excited pace because I was excited when I wrote. I was discovering, pressed by some violent mood. The lines were short, *not* studied" (IWWP, 15). A few years earlier, in his essay on *Leaves of Grass*, he had written of the organic origin of rhythmic units, "We are reminded that the origin of our verse was the dance—and even if it had not been the dance, the heart when it is stirred has multiple beats, and verse at its most impassioned sets the heart violently beating. But as the heart picks up we also begin to count. Finally, the measure for each language and environment is accepted" (ELG, 23). This belief in the origin of verse rhythms in the dance motivated his selection for the cover of *Al Que Quiere!* (1917). As his *I Wanted to Write a Poem* states, "The figure on the cover was taken from a design on a pebble. To me the design looked like a dancer, and the effect of the dancer was very important—a natural, completely individual pattern" (IWWP, 18). The variability of the heartbeat like the natural irregularity of the pebble design allowed Williams to mirror (that is, double) their paces in the free verse of his early volumes.

Yet, as Williams was to announce in his essay on *Leaves of Grass,* he probably never felt completely innocent using free verse: "How could verse be free without being immoral? There is something to it. . . . For as the English had foreseen, this freedom of which there had been so much talk had to have limits somewhere. If not, it would lead you astray. That was the problem. And there was at about that time a whole generation of Englishmen . . . whom it did lead astray in moral grounds. . . . For in your search for freedom—which is desirable—you must stop somewhere, but where exactly shall you stop? Whitman could not say" (ELG, 24, 26). Since mythic patterns of thought have their negative as well as positive manifestations, such fears are not unusual. The figure of the double could as easily lead to destruction as to success. "America, Whitman, and the Art of Poetry" (1917) had insisted: "The only freedom a poet can have is to be conscious of his manoeuvres, to recognize whither he is trending and to govern his sensibilities, his mind, his will so that it accord delicately with his emotions." Free verse was a "misnomer," Williams went on; "It must be truly democratic, truly free for all—and yet it must be governed." [25]

For Williams the first stop and first step away from descent-return structures, "controlled measure," came in 1924 as a result of three separate "discoveries." The first of these was the impact of Eliot's *The Waste Land* (1922), which had managed to deplete the ranks of the Imagists, making free verse less popular. Williams notes in his essay on *Leaves of Grass:* "I shall never forget the impression created by *The Waste Land;* it was as if the bottom had dropped out of everything. I had not known how much the spirit of Whitman animated us until it was withdrawn from us. Free verse became overnight a thing of the past. Men went about congratulating themselves as upon the disappearance of something that had disturbed their dreams; and indeed it was so—the dreams of right-thinking students of English verse had long been disturbed by the appearance among them of the horrid specter of Whitman's free verse. Now it was as if a liberator, a Saint George, had come just in the nick of time to save them. The instructors in all the secondary schools were grateful" (ELG, 24). Elsewhere, his *Autobiography* notes of the work's publication: "These were the years before the great catastrophe to our letters—the appearance of T. S. Eliot's *The Waste Land.* . . . Our work staggered to a halt for a moment under the blast of Eliot's genius which gave the poem back to the academics. We did not know how to answer him. . . . To me especially it struck like a sardonic

28

bullet. I felt at once that it had set me back twenty years, and I'm sure it did [a reference to his own formal poems in *Poems* (1909) and *The Tempers* (1913)]. Critically Eliot returned us to the classroom just at the moment when I felt that we were on the point of an escape to matters much closer to the essence of a new art form itself—rooted in the locality which should give it fruit. I knew at once that in certain ways I was most defeated" (A, 146, 174).

"Eliot," Williams continues, "had turned his back on the possibility of reviving my world. And being an accomplished craftsman, better skilled in some ways than I could ever hope to be, I had to watch him carry my world off with him, the fool, to the enemy" (A, 174). Indications of the "disaster" had been adumbrated already in the Prologue to *Kora* where Williams scores Edgar Jepson's praise of "The Love Song of J. Alfred Prufrock": "Eliot's more exquisite work is rehash, repetition in another way of Verlaine, Baudelaire, Maeterlinck—conscious or unconscious." He explained the Englishman's reaction by asserting that "Eliot is a subtle conformist" (I, 24). Yet it was precisely the occasion of *The Waste Land* that permitted him to go on in 1924 to a poetics based upon imitation and not upon mirroring, though indication of the direction is already evident in *Spring and All*. As he relates the discovery in his *Autobiography*, "This story [concerning Alanson Hartpence's statement that painting is paint] marks the exact point in the transition that took place, in the world of that time, from the appreciation of a work of art as a copying of nature to the thought of it as the imitation of nature, spoken of by Aristotle in his *Poetics*, which has since governed our conceptions" (A, 240). He compares this rediscovered "imitation" to the work of Paul Cézanne and Georges Braque and notes further: "It is NOT to hold the mirror up to nature that the artist performs his work. It is to make, out of the imagination, something not at all a copy of nature, a thing advanced and apart from it" (A, 241). He concludes, "To imitate nature involves the verb to do. To copy is merely to reflect something already there, inertly: Shakespeare's mirror is all that is needed for it. But by imitation we enlarge nature itself, we become nature or we discover in ourselves nature's active part. This is enticing to our minds, it enlarges the concept of art, dignifies it to a place not yet fully realized" (A, 241). Hence, rather than "double" by the old mirroring of surfaces, one now "doubles" by mirroring what is equivalent to a Hegelian *Geist*.

Events other than Hartpence's statement had prepared Williams years earlier for the transition. Marsden Hartley's "Dissertation on Modern Painting" (1921) had denigrated mirroring in almost identical terms, and his *Adventures in the Arts* (1921), cited in *Spring and All*, devotes an entire chapter to Whitman and Cézanne. An idol of the "291" group that Williams joined after 1913, Cézanne had been celebrated by him in *The Egoist* (1915), and his poem, "To a Solitary Disciple" (1916), bears strong evidence of budding cubist tendencies. In 1916, the styles of both Hartley and Charles Demuth underwent alterations that brought them closer to the French painters, and the younger Stuart Davis' experiments in "multiple views" produced *Gloucester Terrace* and what eventually became the frontispiece of *Kora*. Still, "America, Whitman, and the Art of Poetry" uses J. M. W. Turner as its model artist and suggests that in 1917 Williams was not yet fully committed to the new manner. The lateness of Braque's emergence in Paris as a leading modern artist with an identity of his own may have contributed to the date that Williams assigns to the Hartpence story, but "Seventy Years Deep" suggests a more plausible explanation. There Williams notes, "When my wife and I were first married we made a vow that no matter what should occur, after ten years we would follow Sir William Osler's advice and take a year off and go abroad to study. When finally the ten years had elapsed we carried out our plan, even though it meant leaving our two boys—aged seven and nine—at home." [26] That in retrospect he should associate a new artistic beginning with this personal disjunction is natural.

Such a change from copying to imitation did not involve a change in the writer's view of nature, but rather a recognition that the art work has an organic life contained within it as well as an organic relation with the life about it. This recognition led Williams to the further discovery that free verse is "rime" (in other words, a shaper of content). In "This Florida: 1924," he calls it "the stupidest rime of all" since it ignores the necessity of the art work's inner life: "And we thought to escape rime / by imitation of the senseless / unarrangement of wild things— / the stupidest rime of all" (CEP, 330). The effect of the change is apparent in such poems as "Silence" (1944), "The Dish of Fruit" (1945), and "The Flower" (1948). For each, the function of the opening line is to act as a frame that abruptly separates the poem from life. In imitation of a Cézanne painting, the first poem layers blocks of sky, red, yellow, and green, and beneath them posits the outlines of a bird, twig, and peach tree. Like a Braque still life, the

31

second moves from an arrangement of table to poem to dish
of fruit. After beginning with "This too I love," the last
again moves to locate spatially wife, rose, and canary.

That Williams should move to painting for his recovery
from the collapse of Imagism is not surprising. A number
of his friends at this time were painters and, as he told
Edith Heal, "You must remember I had a strong inclina-
tion all my life to be a painter. Under different circumstances I would rather have been a painter than to bother
with these god-damn words" (IWWP, 29). Walter Sutton's
"A Visit with William Carlos Williams" (1961) repeats the
emphasis. Williams tells Sutton: "The image of a painting
identified the man as a poet to me. . . . And as I've grown
older, I've attempted to fuse the poetry and painting to
make it the same thing. . . . I don't care whether it's
representational or not. But to give a design. A design in
the poem and a design in the picture should make them
more or less the same thing." [27] Yet, by reason of the sentimentalism obtaining in introspection, the discovery of the
inner life of the art work does not evoke, except for patterns of thinking, a corresponding emphasis on the inner
life of man and a discovery of his *Geist* away from action.
Williams still believes that such introspection falsifies. A
flatness, a "lateral sliding" on a physical plane, rather than
penetration, marks these poems, recalling James's statement that "it *may* be that some parts of the world are connected so loosely with some other parts as to be strung
along by nothing but the copula *and*." [28] Descents here-
after become less common; yet, in no instance does the
"lateral sliding" exclude "subjective" material so long as
such material contributes instrumentally to action. Williams explains to Sutton: "I was tremendously involved

32

in an appreciation of Cézanne. He was a designer. He put it down on the canvas so that there would be a meaning without saying anything at all. Just the relation of the parts to themselves." [29]

The combination of the effects of *The Waste Land*, the discovery of imitation as the basis of poetry, and the rejection of free verse permits Williams after his meeting with Louis Zukofsky in 1928 to formulate the principles of Objectivism to justify the language and rhythmic units of the new, nondescending poems. Mike Weaver documents part of the drift toward the new poetics in *William Carlos Williams: The American Background* (1971). Citing the influence of the mathematician John Riordan, he is able to date the change in Williams' thought to at least as early as 1925. Riordan, who was a member of A. R. Orage's writing class in New York, introduced the poet first to Charles P. Steinmetz's *Four Lectures on Relativity and Space* (1923) and later to Whitehead's *Science and the Modern World* (1925). From Steinmetz, Williams was to learn something of the nature of the relativity of length and duration. Steinmetz described how two people measuring a standing train and track—one inside the train and the other outside—would get the same results. If they were to check, their watches, too, would agree. However, were the train in full motion, the man outside would find its length grown shorter whereas his counterpart inside would find the length equal to what it had been while standing; yet, for him the track would have grown shorter. If the two were then to compare watches, that of the man inside would appear slow to the one outside whereas the man inside the train would find the watch of the other slow. Stop the train, and their measurements would again agree.

Steinmetz asks, "What then is the 'true' length of the train and the 'true' time—that which I get when measuring the train while it passes me at high speed or that which you get while moving with the train? Both, and neither. It means that length is not a fixed and invariable property of a body, but depends on the conditions under which it is observed." [30]

In Whitehead's chapter on "The Romantic Reaction," Williams encountered the variables of "subjective" and "objective" perception. Whitehead there defined the "objectivist" position as holding "that the things experienced and the cognizant subject enter into the common world on equal terms." [31] In so doing, he rejected the positions of both the subjectivists and intermediate subjectivists that "the nature of . . . immediate experience is the outcome of the perceptive peculiarities of the subject enjoying the experience" and "that the things experienced only indirectly enter into the common world by reason of their dependence on the subject who is cognising." [32] Still, Williams' work shows no indication that he understood the complexities of Steinmetz's space system, especially in regard to metrics and projective geometry, and Zukofsky, who gave the movement its name, disclaims any connection of it to Whitehead's philosophical "objectivism." Weaver is finally forced to conclude that perhaps only Williams of the original Objectivist group had read Whitehead by the time the term was adopted and that any connection between it and the philosopher was Williams' own. Similarly, Williams' later acceptance of Charles Olson's "projective verse" may well be seen as a harkening back to a desire to understand and accept Steinmetz, but this acceptance falls far short of the necessary understanding of "field," and both Williams and Olson proceed from a concept of point space specifically cautioned against by Steinmetz.

Regardless of how indebted at this time one wishes to believe Williams' understanding of Objectivism was to Riordan and these two thinkers, his understanding of its principles and the way it would relate to his earlier work in the *Autobiography* is clear: "But, we argued, the poem, like every other form of art, is an object, an object that in itself formally presents its case and its meaning by the very form it assumes. Therefore, being an object, it should be so treated and controlled—but not as in the past. For past objects have about them past necessities—like the sonnet —which have conditioned them and from which, as a form itself, they cannot be freed" (A, 264–265). "The poem," he insists, "being an object (like the symphony or cubist painting) it must be the purpose of the poet to make of his words a new form: to invent, that is, an object consonant with his day" (A, 265). The relationships of the Orphean song and not the process of the Orphean descent and return become the subject matter; the world sung becomes by the very fact of the song different from the world unsung. Here Steinmetz's description of the difference between mathematical and physical space bears most relevantly on both modern art and Williams. Three points may be all that are needed to locate a plane in mathematics, but in physical space at least six data or coordinates are necessary; in addition to the three points of mathematics three other determinants are needed to fix the relationship of the viewer and body in space. Such a realization on Williams' part permits him to say of his early poems when he assembled them for *Collected Poems 1921–1931* (1934): "I could reject the looseness of the free verse. Free verse wasn't verse at all to me. All art is orderly" (IWWP, 65).

Yet by virtue of its being a rhyme that ignored the intrinsic form of the art work for fidelity to an artist's somatic excitement, the verse bore a residual orderliness, conventionalism, and academicism that "disturbed" him: "My models, Shakespeare, Milton, dated back to a time when men thought in an orderly fashion. I felt that modern life had gone beyond that; our poems could not be contained in the strict orderliness of the classics" (IWWP, 65). Thus as a consequence of the collapse of Imagism and free verse, Williams was forced to confront anew one of his life's recurrent major problems, that of finding the right structure for poetry. This structure would relate to life and at the same time realize the organic ontology of poetic rhythm and provide it with controls. Only briefly would he be armed with mathematics. From 1928 to 1931, he engaged in a series of attacks on science, philosophy, and religion. What he was looking for in the alliance of rhythmic units to language could not be found simply in abstract mathematics. It must lie now, too, in the equivalency of the sea surface and depth that had replaced the mirror as a metaphor of his poetics. In this equivalency, the manner in which the present (surface) would embrace the dreams of one's youth (depth) would be consistent with contemporary notions of thought process.

In Section III of *Paterson II* (1948), Williams claims to have found his answer in still another remove from Steinmetz. The answer lay both in an interplay of a triadic line and a variable foot and in a return mentally to the mythic

Orphean patterns of his Imagist period: "The descent beckons / as the ascent beckoned / Memory is a kind / of accomplishment / a sort of renewal / even / an initiation" (P, 96). Earlier, *Paterson I* (1946) had returned him to the Passaic "baptism" of "The Wanderer," and almost coevally, "The Old House" (1948) added its own descent-return structure to the revival. Using Steinmetz's terminology, Williams seems to disregard the mathematician's warning that "measurements and dimensional relations . . . are not rigidly possible in physical space, and strictly, we cannot speak of the length or the size of a body, as we cannot measure it by bringing the measure to it, because the length and shape of the measure change when it is moved through space." [33] Williams tells of his discovery in *I Wanted to Write a Poem:* "Several years afterward in looking over the thing I realized I had hit upon a device (that is the practical focus of a device) which I could not name when I wrote it. My dissatisfaction with free verse came to a head in that I always wanted a verse that was ordered, so it came to me that the concept of the foot itself would have to be altered in our new relativistic world" (IWWP, 82). By his own admission, it took several years to frame the concept so that it might allow the inclusion of organic units: "The foot not being fixed is only to be described as variable. If the foot itself is variable it allows order in so-called free verse. Thus the verse becomes not free at all but just simply variable, as all things in life properly are. . . . Now I had it—a sea change. The verse must be coldly, intellectually considered. Not the emotion, the heat of life dominating, but the intellectual concept of the thing itself" (IWWP, 82–83). But a reader of Williams' Introduction to Byron Vazakas' *Transfigured Night* (1946) might see there already, in another context, the seeds of the awareness.

Focusing on the younger poet's completely having "done away with the poetic line as we know it," Williams speaks of his invention of "a workable expedient to replace it. He has found a *measure* based not upon convention, but upon music . . . , a measure that is inviolable to the old attack. He abandoned an eye habit with all its stale catch, threw all that aside for pure ear." "Furthermore," Williams notes, "by returning to music, whence poetry came, . . . Vazakas has at the same time made a transit from English . . . to our own spoken tongue, freeing that to its own melodies." [34] Earlier, he had described the typography of Vazakas' quadratic structure as "something like a toy cannon, a long top sticking out to the left, over a base of three shorter ones. . . . It isn't a line. Nor is it a stanza, for a stanza is made up of a series of lines, and this had none. It isn't prose because it is so definitely a measure. . . . What we have wanted is a *line* that will allow us room in which to develop the opportunities of a new language, a line loose as Whitman's but *measured* as his was not." "The thing to notice about this more or less accidental discovery of Vazakas," he continues, "is that it has a very definite regularity resembling, however vaguely, a musical bar. A bar, definitely, since it is not related to grammar, but to time. . . . The clause, the sentence, and the paragraph are ignored, and the progression goes over into the next bar as much as the musical necessity requires . . . a sequence of musical bars arranged vertically on the page, and capable of infinite modulation." [35] At the time, Williams was already writing *Paterson,* and engaged in fusing

38

his current knowledge with the dreams of his younger years along the lines of art, where even Weaver concedes the poet had retreated after his encounter with Steinmetz. Nonetheless, in the growing autotelism of his turn toward memory, his triadic version of this variable measure would become more and more important in his efforts to overcome the new psychically "hopeless and desperate situations" motivating first "Asphodel," then *Paterson V*, and finally "Pictures from Brueghel."

CHAPTER TWO

Paterson: The Dream Extended

⅏ If the poetry of William Carlos Williams was to pass through a kind of cubism in the twenties and thirties, it is out of this cubism that the clearest understanding of both these early short poems and the total structure of *Paterson* emerges. At least insofar as technique is concerned, the long poem represents the first of three extended efforts of the poet during his late years to build upon the achievements of these early works. Wylie Sypher's *Rococo to Cubism in Art and Literature* associates the art movement with the scientific relativism of F. H. Bradley, Albert Einstein, and Alfred North Whitehead: "The cubist world is the world of a new physics," of a reality "that . . . can have no absolute contours but varies with the angle from which one sees it." [1] Its various perspectives as they reflect the plurality of identities common to pragmatism define the identity of things as the views one takes of them, or, as Whitehead later called it, one's "prehensions" of them. Yet, as Clement Greenberg's *Art and Culture* suggests, the very alteration in the composition of an art work which cubism produces can lead to serious new problems regarding perspective: "By that time, flatness had not only invaded but was threatening to swamp the Cubist picture. The little facet-planes into which Braque and Picasso were dissecting everything visible now all lay parallel to the picture plane. They were no longer controlled, either in drawing or in placing, by linear or even scalar perspective. Each facet tended to be shaded, moreover, as an independent unit, with no legato passages, no unbroken tracts of value gradation on its open side, to join it to adjacent facet-planes." [2] "The main problem at this juncture," he explains, "became to keep the 'inside' of the picture—its content—from fusing with the 'outside'—its literal surface. *Depicted* flatness—that is, the facet-planes had to be kept separate enough from *literal* flatness to permit a minimal illusion of three-dimensional space to survive between the two." [3]

One early variation on their discovery was the simultaneism of Robert Delaunay which, in *The Hieroglyphics of a New Speech* (1969), Bram Dijkstra describes as influencing such of Williams' works as *Kora in Hell* (1920). The opening issue of *291* (1915) had defined the technique as "the simultaneous representation of the different figures of a form seen from different points of view, as Picasso or Braque did some time ago; or—the simultaneous representation of the figure of several forms, as the futurists are doing." [4] Dijkstra assigns the automatic writing of Williams' book as well as the stress on simultaneity and the number of references to painters in its Prologue to the poet's aligning "his work with that of the painters." [5] He goes on to note that "Williams did not have any . . . doubts about the viability of simultaneity of poetry. He took his cue from the manner in which objects were juxtaposed at will in certain paintings by Delaunay and others, and proceeded to do with language what they were doing with paint." [6] In the work, words succeed each other, each occupying a place in time. Coevally, thoughts and reactions to sense impressions occur. "By barraging the reader with a non-logically constructed sequence of direct sense impressions, and by combining the thoughts or the voices of three or four people within a specific instant of time in an inconsequential sequence," Dijkstra observes, "the poet will succeed in breaking the impression of the flow of time. Each sentence becomes a separate 'object.' " [7] The result is a "polyphony of simultaneous voices," which in 291 the anonymous author associates with simultaneism.

This "polyphony" was what the painter Stuart Davis was trying to accomplish with his own compositions at approximately the same time. These compositions, Williams' *I Wanted to Write a Poem* (1958) asserts, were doing "graphically exactly what I was trying to do in words" (IWWP, 29). H. H. Aranson's introduction to the *Stuart Davis Memorial Exhibition* points out that "of greatest significance at this period is a series of paintings in which the artist applies his newly found strong and arbitrary color, his sense of brush stroke and of space organization to fragmented subject matter in which an accumulation of separate visual details is reorganized in a new reality of paint surface. The individual details are not as yet dismembered in the cubist manner . . . but there is already implicit . . . the artist's mature approach to the problems of illusion, reality, abstraction." [8] "On clear days," Davis recalls, "the air and water had a brilliance of light greater than I had ever seen. While this tended to destroy local color, it stimulated the desire to invent high intensity color intervals." [9] These "high intensity color intervals" lie at the heart of simultaneism. As early as 1839, a chemistry professor, Michel-Eugène Chevreul had put forth in his very influential *De la Loi du contraste simultané des couleurs* a theory of two kinds of color harmony, one of similarity and the other of contrast.

In Chevreul's system, simultaneousness is the consequence of "two or more colors which are perceived simultaneously by the eye and thereupon commence an action based on definite laws." [10] As summarized in Max Imdahl's "Delaunay's Position in History," these laws propose that "harmony of similarity occurs when two related colors, such as red and red-orange, of identical tone level [intensity] appear side by side, or when two related tone levels of one and the same red value appear side by side. Harmony of contrast occurs when two colors, related or even identical in quality but of the most different tone level, appear side by side." More impressive than the contrast of tone in two related colors is the effect of two complementary colors' being side by side, especially when identical tone levels serve to increase the contrast effect. Disharmony, Chevreul proposes, "occurs when two colors which are neither similar nor in complementary contrast with each other are seen side by side, such as red and yellow. To see such colors simultaneously is irritating to the eye." [11]

As Delaunay's "Notes on Painting" (1912) reaffirmed, "Simultaneous contrast is the dynamic of colors, and it is also their construction, meaning depth, uneven measures, and it is the strongest means of expressing reality. . . . Simultaneity of colors by means of simultaneous contrasts and all measures (uneven) evolved from colors, according to their visible movement—this is the only reality which

43

painting can construct." [12] The "dynamic" to which Delaunay alludes is the illusion which simultaneous contrast creates by exaggerating color differences. For example, a light object appears lighter next to a dark object and, conversely, the dark object takes on a darker appearance. Green next to red will appear greener; orange next to blue more orange; and violet next to yellow more violet. These may, in turn, have something to do with the "contending forces" which, in *Kora,* Williams has producing a "picture of perfect rest," for their movement upon one another produces the lines separating both. At Gloucester, Davis found his equivalent—"the necessary element to his thinking coherently about art"—in the schooner. Its masts defined the often empty sky expanse and, as he learned, functioned "as a color-space coordinate between earth and sky. They make it possible for the novice landscape painter to evade the dangers of 'taking off' into the void as soon as his eye hits the horizon." [13] From the masts of these schooners, Davis eventually learned—"when for some unavoidable reason they were not present"—to invent his own coordinates. Still, color alone, however much it might add to the dynamic of a canvas, could not get one out of the problem of flatness that the perspective of cubism raised.

As a way out of the problem, Braque and Picasso jointly hit upon the notion of the collage where, as Greenberg records, "the illusion of depth created by the contrast between the affixed material and everything else gives way immediately to an illusion of forms in bas-relief, which gives way in turn, and with equal immediacy, to an illusion that seems to contain both—or neither." [14] His collage technique, which art historians grant as a major turning point in the evolution both of cubism and of modernist art, marks the shift from analytical to synthetic cubism though, as Greenberg insists, synthetic cubism did not fully begin there. He places its beginning when Picasso carried "the forward push of the collage (and of Cubism in general) *literally* into the literal space in front of the picture plane." [15] Picasso did this by cutting and folding a piece of paper in the shape of a guitar and gluing and fitting to it four taut strings and other pieces of paper. He created thereby a sequence of "flat surfaces in real and sculptured space to which there clung only the vestige of a picture plane." [16]

This new dimensionality, while in no way returning to the fixed point of perspective, proves the cubist's ability to assimilate into his pictorial world at the precise point where art and nature intersect elements of actuality previously alien to painting. He has, in short, moved art space into life space. It remained for the Spanish painter, Juan Gris, to carry on the technique of the collage after it had been abandoned by its inventors. Davis' solution in the "imitated" collage was different. E. C. Goossen's *Stuart Davis* points out that "by imitating rather than actually using the labels of such things as cigarette packages, etc., Davis destroyed, in one sense, the essence of collage, but freed himself from the limitations of the size of the objects." [17] The imitation reaffirmed the plane of the canvas as the place where the picture occurs and led eventually to another sort of solution in abstraction. Nonetheless, if the image of this relative universe could cause such invention, division, and conflicts in the arrangements of perspective in art, it would also cause certain division and conflicts in a poet whose *Kora in Hell* asserted that the space of poetry involved a cycle of descent and return, where "at the sickening turn toward death the pieces are joined into a pretty thing . . . art . . . a thing to carry up with you on the next turn" (I, 71). Williams, too, might need something as drastic as the collage as he moved toward cubism, if his art were to lose the flatness inherent there.

In *Spring and All* (1923), a basically simultaneist work, Williams, as if anticipating the future needs of his art, gives over a section of the prose to a discussion of Gris's techniques. He especially praises Gris's practice of using real objects *literally* in his collages: "Here is a shutter, a bunch of grapes, a sheet of music, a picture of sea and mountains (particularly fine) which the onlooker is not for a moment permitted to witness as an 'illusion' " (I, 110). Daniel-Henry Kahnweiler's *Juan Gris, His Life and His Work* recalls that "even in the early days, in 1912, he used pages from books and pieces of mirror in his pictures; but whereas, with Picasso in particular, the newspaper was often used simply as a piece of material, with Gris the fragment of mirror represents a mirror, the printed book page is itself, and so is the piece of newspaper. . . . 'You want to know why I had to stick on a piece of mirror?' he said to [Michel] Leiris. 'Well, surfaces can be re-created and volumes interpreted in a picture, but what is one to do about a mirror whose surface is always changing and which should reflect even the spectator? There is nothing else to do but stick on a real piece.' " [18] Williams repeats the praise in letters to Charles Henri Ford (1930) and Kay Boyle (1932), as well as in his *Autobiography* (1951) and *A Novelette and Other Prose (1921–1931)* (1932). To Ford, he admits, "That man was my perfect artist." [19] From Kay Boyle, he wants to know, "Why do we not read more of

Juan Gris? He knew these things [how art form is intrinsic in the times] in painting and wrote well of them" (SL, 130). This last is most likely an allusion to Gris's "Des Possibilités de la Peinture" (1924), the last part of which appeared in the *Transatlantic Review* in an issue containing the Mayflower section of Williams' *In the American Grain* (1925).

Yet the two poems that Williams constructs to accompany his discussion and endorsement of Gris in *Spring and All,* like his earlier cubist poem "To a Solitary Disciple" (1916), in no way affix "real" objects to their surfaces, however much they may realize the effects of Gris's method, described by Williams in prose: "One thing laps over on the other, the cloud laps over the shutter, the bunch of grapes is part of the handle of the guitar, the mountain and sea are obviously not 'the mountain and sea,' but a picture of the mountain and the sea. All drawn with admirable simplicity and excellent design—all a unity" (I, 110–111). His first poem, entitled "The Rose" in *The Collected Earlier Poems* (1951), is, as Dijkstra points out, based on Gris's collage *Roses* (1914): "The roses are photographic, cut out of a flower catalogue perhaps, or from a poster, and literally pasted into the composition. Williams, by his own admission, saw only a black and white reproduction of this collage, and in black and white the fact that this work is a collage is obscured." [20] The poem describes the "fragility of the flower / unbruised" which "penetrates space," but the work itself does not penetrate space by similarly affixing the shape of a literal flower to its surface. Likewise, in approximating cubist displacement, "At the Faucet of June" (1923) makes no advance toward synthetic cubism. While more like Braque, "The Dish of

Fruit" (1945) in *The Collected Later Poems* (1950) in no way furthers the poem as cubist experience. A description of an object is not the process of a multilevel perception of it; the cubist subject matter of these poems simply does not make them cubist in execution.

If one were to consider two kinds of prose, two kinds of poetry, or prose and poetry as two different facet-planes because of their different moods or different densities, one might argue that the text and commentary of *Kora* which vacillates between roman and italic type, or "The Testament of Perpetual Change" (1948) which carries on the same vacillation in poetry, or the text and prose of *Spring and All* or "The Descent of Winter" (1928) might be considered cubist, albeit their stresses on simultaneism would make them at best a kind of analytical rather than synthetic cubism. This seems to be the position of Williams, who in a chapter of "A Novelette" entitled "Juan Gris" remarks: "[Ezra] Pound will say that the improvisations [that is, *Kora in Hell*] are . . . twenty, forty years late. On the contrary . . . their excellence is, in major part, the shifting of category. It is the disjointing process" (I, 285). Still, that would make a work like Dante's *La vita nuova,* based upon a similar mixture of prose and poetry, a proto-cubist work, as would be Giordano Bruno's *Heroic Frenzies* and Petronius' *Satyricon.* And if John C. Thirlwall's "William Carlos Williams' *Paterson*" (1961) is correct in spotting Williams' ultimate indebtedness not to Chaucer's *Canterbury Tales* but to an early reading of *Aucassin and Nicolette,* this work becomes proto-cubist as well. Georges Lemaître's *From Cubism to Surrealism in French Literature* is willing to entertain such notions

48

about painting when it makes cubist art relatable to medieval multiple depictions of saints' lives.

Yet there is another element of cubism, its reduction of shapes to geometric forms, which must also be considered. One cannot dismiss Paul Cézanne's oft-quoted statement, "Represent nature by means of the cylinder, the sphere, the cone," or the cubist's tendency to "destroy" objects by reshaping them into intelligent "pictorial facts." Williams attempts this destruction in *A Voyage to Pagany* (1928). He describes a Paris *asile* as "low gray houses ranged around in a hexagonal symmetry . . . [that] said Braque. It linked completely with the modern spirit . . . cold, gray, dextrous, multiform, and yet gracious" (VP, 39). But the language of geometry is not geometry and, here, one might find the equation of a work of literature with cubist art hardest to hold, although one might argue that Williams' reduction of thoughts to their nonsentimental expressions may be a suitable verbal equivalent to the reduction of objects to their geometric shapes. Nevertheless, the point is that, however impossible it may be to translate cubist art into cubist poetry, Williams clearly conceived the problems of dimensionality in poetry to be similar to the problems of dimensionality in cubism and sought, however wrong-headedly, to solve these problems by poetic equivalents of paint. Nor was he alone in his belief in the interrelatedness of poetry and cubism. There was Guillaume Apollinaire; and, as Kahnweiler points out, Gris in the *Open Windows* series, used by Williams for his example in *Spring and All*, was himself trying to translate painting into "poetry."

For Apollinaire, who abandons traditional punctuation

and emphasizes the obscure, the disjointed, and the jerky in the verse of *Alcools* (1913), a mystical element lay in the dissolving surfaces and attempts to seize "l'univers infini comme idéal." The element is not common to Williams or Gris, but it informs the work of poets like E. E. Cummings, Archibald MacLeish, and Kenneth Rexroth, and it affords the basis of what is normally considered "cubist poetry." Gris's own "poetry" was another matter. Kahnweiler describes it as "signs" which Gris used as "emblems": "They *are* a knife or a glass. They are never symbols, for they never have a dual identity. . . . They *are* the objects which they represent, with all the emotive values attaching to them; but they never signify anything outside of these objects." By their repetition in one or a sequence of paintings these signs become "rhymes" which "reveal to the beholder certain hidden relationships, similarities between two apparently different objects." "In 1920," Kahnweiler notes, "these metaphors are fairly evident and are based on the simplest objects (playing cards, glasses, etc.). Then a bunch of grapes is compared to a mandolin (1921). Finally, objects of increasingly disparate character are reconciled through more inventive 'rhymes.' In the *Portrait of a Woman* of 1922, for example, the woman's head is repeated in her hand. In *The Nun* of 1922, the whole figure is repeated in reverse in the clasped hands and the folds of the sleeves. In *Three Masks* of 1923, the rhymes have become still more numerous and the head of each figure is repeated in the folds of their garments, their arms, etc." [21]

To complete these "rhymes," Gris altered but never abandoned Cézanne's famous pronunciamento. As he wrote for *L'Esprit Nouveau* (1921), he wanted to "humanize" art:

"Cézanne turns a bottle into a cylinder, but I begin with a cylinder and create an individual of a special type: I make a bottle—a particular bottle—out of a cylinder." [22] In the *Transatlantic Review*, he describes the result in terms of a weaving metaphor: "Painting for me is like a fabric, all of a piece and uniform, with one set of threads as the representational, or abstract element, and the cross-threads as the technical, architectural, or abstract element. These threads are interdependent and complementary, and if one set is lacking the fabric does not exist." [23] Williams' "A Novelette" translates this image of warp and woof into the crossthreads of novelistic conversation and novelistic design: "Always the one thing in Juan Gris. Conversation as design. Were it not so—it is less than actual, it is covered, dull, a makeshift. I have always admired and partaken of Juan Gris. Singly he says that the actual is the drawing of the face—and so the face borrowing of the drawing—by lack of copying and lack of a burden to the story—is real" (I, 286).

In "Marianne Moore" (1925), Williams discusses the appearance of this "fabric" in poetry: "The interstices for the light and not the interstitial web of the thought concerned her, or so it seems to me. Thus the material is as the handling: the thought, the word, the rhythm—all in the style. The effect is in the penetration of the light itself, how much, how little; the appearance of the luminous background" (SE, 128). Or, as he says in more practical terms, "There are two elements essential to Miss Moore's scheme of composition, the hard and unaffected concept of the apple itself as an idea, then its edge-to-edge contact with the things which surround it. . . . The thought is used exactly as the apple, it is the same insoluble block" (SE,

127, 130). A second essay on Miss Moore, published in 1948, makes the association of her and the cubists even more explicit: "Miss Moore has taken recourse to the mathematics of art. Picasso does no different: a portrait is a stratagem singularly related to a movement among the means of the craft. By making these operative, relationships become self-apparent" (SE, 293).

This translation of art problems into poetry allows words to take on some of the characteristics which pigments in cubist painting took on as it moved toward synthetic cubism and, under Braque and Picasso, began to thicken its paints with sand or ashes. As Kahnweiler notes, "This 'solidification' of the color was intended to diminish the viscous appearance of oil paint and so restrict the possibility of virtuosity in the execution. . . . The painters of 1912 felt that the medium created by the painters of the fifteenth century was no longer adequate to their purpose, which was so radically different from the Renaissance." [24] Comparably, having described how for Miss Moore "a word is a word most when it is separated out by science, treated with acid to remove the smudges, washed, dried and placed right side up on a clean surface," Williams goes on to note, "It may be used not to smear it again with thinking (the attachments of thought) but in such a way that it will remain scrupulously itself, clean perfect, unnicked beside other words in parade" (SE, 128–129). This "solidification," which is anticipated by his assertion that "particles of language must be clear as sand" (IAG, 221) and by his generally "cubist" remarks on Edgar Allan Poe in *In the American Grain,* he makes a part of Miss Moore's modernity. It is the reduction of Dante's "illustrious" and consequently fourfold symbolizing language of *De vulgari eloquentia* to something more worldly, and reinforces his even earlier emphasis in his Prologue to *Kora* on language's true rather than associational or sentimental value.

The solidification of words also permitted language to act as color in the color harmonies of a work; but, just as it had been the problem of dimensionality that finally forced the cubists to invent the collage, so it proved to be the problem of dimensionality joined to return that finally forced Williams into the synthetic innovations of *Paterson*, for it was not until he began to incorporate items from newspapers and segments of historical documents and letters that one can say that art space begins to intrude on life space and the collage begins. This intrusion, the reverse of the "background effects" of quotations in Pound's *Cantos* and T. S. Eliot's *The Waste Land*, comes after other experiments with dimensionality, and it is with these that one should perhaps begin. Yet, as with his poems generally, the degree to which the success of these experiments depends upon the writer's intention and not upon the unconscious elements present will, for the moment, remain unexplored.

Language, syntax, punctuation, spacing, setting, shifts in voice, tense, mood, and thought, for example, constitute the traditional shapes of dimensionality in Williams' early poems. The reader accordingly moves from life into and through the art work and returns to life. This process, which approximates the Kora myth and the process of poetry described in *Kora in Hell*, is apparent in such poems as "A Coronal" (1920). The poem begins with the prediction of fall, of Kora's annual descent into hell. Although set in a future tense, the prediction is based upon regular recurrence rather than upon a novel event and, thus, is stated in the passive voice. The very essence of the voice indicates man's inability to alter the season's course. When one does move into the realm of the controllable and the active voice, a "we" intrudes and an abrupt new facet-plane begins. This emergence is accented by the co-ordinating conjunction "but," which begins the stanza as well as the stanza's shift into a past tense. One moves again immediately in the next line into a new facet-plane as not only a new person is introduced in the impersonal "one" but a new point in futurity is described. This point is past fall, in spring and after the return of Kora, suggested now by the use of the personal pronoun "her." Thus a reader is drawn into a dimensionality created by the poet mainly through time-shifts within a sequence of occurrences which brings him from autumn to spring, from expectation to fulfillment. With this fulfillment the reader is released into the life space he enjoyed before he began reading.

"History" (1917) realizes this process more graphically as it takes its reader from an outside setting into the interior of a museum and then returns him to the outdoors, again much as Kora is taken into hell and then returned to earth. This more obvious use of setting in no way diminishes Williams' handling of shifts in time and person to create facet-planes. It does permit him, however, to add to the predominantly time illusion of "A Coronal" an illusion of space by naming a sequence of objects to convey passage by those objects. Yet it is "To a Solitary Disciple," which, as an early "cubist" work, offers the reader the closest approximation of the problems in dimensionality that Williams had to face. It begins with three disparate concepts kept separate from life by their beginning with "rather" and kept parallel to each other by the repetition of the word. Instead of being an invitation toward descent, as the first word of the poem, "rather" immediately cuts the work off from life, much as a frame cuts off an easel picture from life. The poem goes on to pose alternatives which, like the reverse images in the "poetry" of Gris's paintings, conclude in a series of three unqualified commands to observe. The parallelism that begins with the moon's being opposed to the steeple thus ends with the edifice's being opposed to lightness. Yet in this progress a flatness emerges similar to the flatness of a painting, which may well be what Williams intends to describe. Consequently there is no depth and no descent; the reader remains throughout in the platform space of life, as if the facet-planes that were being created were fusing into the literal flatness of the page. The final observation of the poem, which turns not on life but on the opening observation, forces the reader into a return to life as abrupt as had been his entrance into the work. The lesson has been concluded for the disciple by the master's silence. The same flatness occurs in "The Rose" and "The Dish of Fruit."

Only "At the Faucet of June" among these previously mentioned early "cubist" poems offers an exception. It introduces a dimensionality that reverses the carefully controlled inner descent of "History." Its abrupt assertion of a patch of yellow on a varnished floor is followed by a permissive wandering of the mind, descending, so to speak, into facet-planes that depict the realms of memory and imagination. The wandering ends more ethereally than Williams' poems are wont to conclude, suggesting perhaps the "mystical element" in some kinds of cubism; but the illusion of dimension created by the associational drift through time is clear. Like Kora one can descend through it. "Paterson" (1927), whose "cylindrical trees" and "complex mathematic" suggest even in this early draft that it, too, was intended as a "cubist" poem, moves from spring to winter described so as to remind the reader of spring's return. Similarly it allows a dimensionality of descent and return; yet the descents of none of these poems constitute a noticeable intrusion of art into life.

These early attempts at cubism occur in works that are entirely poetic, and *Paterson* deliberately chooses to shape its dimensionality to a mixture of prose and poetry. As such, it recurs most clearly to the dreams surrounding the alternating prose and poetry of *Spring and All* and "The Descent of Winter." Despite dadaist touches, the first of these most nearly approximates in discourse the dynamic of what Chevreul's laws of color might term "the harmony of contrasts." Just as light objects appear lighter next to dark objects and aligned complementary colors produce an impression that both colors are purer and more vibrant, so the interlaced, variously sized segments of prose and poetry allow the two forms to appear more purely themselves. The flatness of the prose will make the poetry appear more vivid and intense and, conversely, the prose itself will seem argued and subdued. In its effort to be epiphanic, to bring the reader to an awareness of the differences between prose and poetry and the purposes of each, the work concludes with a running discussion of both. Williams points out, for instance, that "some work of Whitman's is bad poetry and some, in the same meter [though not necessarily by Whitman] is prose." Writing on Marianne Moore, he expresses the belief that it is "possible, even essential, that when poetry fails it does not become prose but bad poetry. The test of Marianne Moore would be that she writes sometimes good and sometimes bad poetry but always—with a single purpose out of a single fountain" (I, 145). The total lack of contact between the subject matter of the work's prose and poetry, however, results in a lack of focus and a sense that the overall structure is disunified.

"The Descent of Winter" provides a reader with even greater problems of focus. The work covers a period of autumn beginning just after the autumnal equinox (September 27) and ending just before the winter solstice (December 12). But, whereas *Spring and All* remains generally a contrast of poetry and prose, "Descent" offers up a sort of "artist's sketchbook," whose entries consist more diversely of poems, epigrams, and a mixture of several kinds of prose. Intermixed with literary theory are the experiences of a doctor, and the reader has this new dimension to contend with. Thus, in addition to the problems of the earlier work, one has here contrasts between criticism and autobiography, analysis and narration. This second opposition recalls the contrasting prose sections of *Kora*, where, as both Dijkstra and Joseph N. Riddel have pointed out, words move "between a subjective and an objective language— . . . experience and explanation of experience." Williams' preoccupation with these contrasts instead of with the interplay of nature and art reaffirms his statement in "A Novelette" that writing "is the theme of all I do. It is the writing" (I, 291). It reasserts the analytic rather than synthetic character of the two efforts.

The lack of intrusion into life common to all these pieces may account for the sense of artistic failure which Williams expresses in a letter written to Horace Gregory

(1945) shortly before he began the work of putting together the final version of *Paterson*. That he felt he had
to find a new method for the poem is clear. He mentions
the need to both Gregory and James Laughlin and records
the crisis in his *Autobiography*. To Gregory he writes,
"The old approach is outdated, and I shall have to work
like a fiend to make myself new again. . . . Either I remake myself or I am done. I can't escape the dilemma
longer. THAT is what has stopped me" (SL, 234–235). To
Laughlin he writes of the work's being given over to the
critics, "I hope it cuts their hearts out. It won't; they're too
grooved in their protective tracks ever to turn aside to see
the dulled world close about them—always whistling into
the distance" (SL, 237). To posterity he says of *Paterson,*
"It called for a poetry such as I did not know, it was my
duty to discover or make such a context on the 'thought' "
(A, 392). As indication that this new poetry and new self
had emerged, he asked Laughlin early in 1946 to drop the
Carlos from his signature and to publish him henceforth
as "William Williams." His wife Flossie's objections, however, ended this plan.

That the method Williams decided on is akin not to the
"cubism" he used in many of his earlier works but to a
synthetic cubism is made more apparent by his comments
to Ralph Nash than by any explanation of the poem he
expressly provides. Nash's article, "The Use of Prose in
Paterson" (1953), had separated the poem's prose into three
general categories: newspaper clippings and factual data,
directly transcribed; authorial summaries of historical data,
excerpted from old newspapers, local histories, and so
forth; and personal letters. It had further classified the
materials as prose of contemporary or of historical fact.

Nash had then gone on to note: "I mean this to stress their nature as blocks of material coming into the poem from outside. . . . [A] letter (or anything else) written by someone other than the poet brings into the poem something of an air of documentation. Irrelevancies and private allusions emphasize that this is not exactly a piece of the poem, but a piece of the poet's world." He had then concluded of the device, "No doubt Williams intends it partly as a forceful marriage of his poem's world with that world of reality from which he is fearful of divorcing himself." [25] This marriage is precisely the effect of synthetic cubism and its building art out into life space, and one can understand Williams' enthusiastic response: "When I read, or had read to me, your article on my use of prose in my poem, *Paterson,* I was left speechless. . . . You have penetrated to a secret source of whatever power I possess and it has frightened me. . . . I shall have to study the distinctions you make between your observation of what I have done, for it strikes me as on the whole so just and acute an observation of my style that I still can't believe it" (SL, 323). Still, the "instinctual" nature which he claims for the technique later in the letter cannot be without some degree of "consciousness" if his statements to Gregory and Laughlin are to be believed.

What Williams seems to suggest as instinctual and valuable is Nash's having found integral the poem's prose rhythms: "You have spotted it in my insistence on the use of prose *within the poem itself* [Williams' italics] when I did not see the reasons so clearly and that's why I think it so remarkable" (SL, 324). This has particular reference to Nash's finding in the relationship of prose and poetry a meaningful kind of counterpoint: "It is evident that the prose affects the poem most strongly by its sound, by the inevitable interruption to eye and ear whenever one of the prose passages appears. This means, for one thing, that the prose is of tremendous importance to the pace and tempo of the entire poem. Nowhere is this more striking than in the eight pages of closely set type that provide a tortured, involved, garrulous, intimate, but ultimately dignified and quiet close for Book Two." [26] Earlier Williams had written Parker Tyler (1948) that "all the prose [in *Paterson*], including the tail which would have liked to have wagged the dog, has primarily the purpose of giving a metrical meaning to or of emphasizing a metrical continuity between all word use. It is *not* an antipoetic device. . . . It *is* that prose and verse are both *writing*, both a matter of the words and an interrelation between words for the purpose of exposition, or other better defined purpose of *the art.*" Williams then asserts, "Poetry does not *have* to be kept away from prose as Mr. Eliot might insist, it goes *along with* prose and, companionably, by itself, without aid or excuse or need for separation or bolstering, shows *itself* by itself for what it is" (SL, 263).

Much earlier *Spring and All* had explained that "prose has to do with the fact of an emotion; poetry has to do with the dynamization of emotion into a separate form" (I, 133). "Prose, relieved of extraneous, unrelated values," Williams went on, "must return to its only purpose; to clarify to enlighten the understanding. There is no form to prose but that which depends on clarity. . . . Poetry is something quite different. Poetry has to do with the crystallization of the imagination—the perfection of new forms as additions to nature." He had concluded the discussion with: "Prose may follow to enlighten but poetry"

(I, 140), being an act of the imagination, has an actuating, enlivening "vividness" which prose can only adumbrate. Given the specific factual prose of *Paterson,* none of these earlier distinctions fits. Certainly the prose is not there for the sole purpose of clarification; it tends to complicate and to build independent of and often in contrast to the poetry, clarifying, perhaps, in the metrical sense that both Williams and Nash speak of and in the sense of simultaneism but not in the sense that *Spring and All* defines.

Faced in his *Multiple Views* with the same failures of focus that mar the composition of *Spring and All* and "The Descent of Winter," Davis, too, had gone for aid to the cubists. In the "fragmentation of observed volumetric forms, re-presented as skins and essences pressed flat upon the canvas," Goossen observes, Davis had recorded many views of a subject as one. "Thus the element of time could be captured within a picture." [27] But in order to do this, he selected and defined the spatial limits of his drawings so that he could achieve an objective attitude toward positional relations and then integrated these with color relations so that both might be thought of simultaneously. In the *Eggbeater* series (1927–1928), this meant first the setting up of a still life—here including an eggbeater, an electric fan, and a rubber glove—and then the painting of the objects repeatedly until they ceased to exist in the eye and mind except as color, line, and shape relationships. From naturalistic form one moved to geometrical and then to logical elements. Eventually Davis would go to the "all-over" concept of his murals where, by flooding the wall space to the brim, "he was able to achieve an evenly distributed rhythm quite concordant with the truth about the eye's inability to apprehend huge pictures in any proximal relation." [28] Williams never got so pure or abstract as to leave the natural image; he remained tied by the necessary concreteness of poetic language to, at least, words whose referents evoked specific things.

Williams seems to have gone in part for his solution to the practice of David Lyle. A former radio marine, Lyle had moved to Paterson in 1938 to work at the Wright Aero Factory. The year before, he had discovered what he believed was a link between abstract communications codes like Morse and patterns of human behavior, and he felt that working out the connection might remedy the problems of the world by bringing a proper and complete alignment of thought and fact. He began to send various people letters correlating their writings and printed statements. Williams received his first letter in 1938 and continued to receive and read letters until 1947, when he began to cast them aside unopened. The style of the letters exhibited a system of chance that both attracted and disturbed the poet. Rejecting the logic of narration, Lyle arranged his material across the page in blocks, using indentations to mark where they matched. The correlations turned Williams' attentions to news and a concept of the poem as the truth of contemporary events, but he rearranged Lyle's patterns by restoring chronology to the incidents and reconstructing the texts so that they followed the appearance of a single, uninterrupted stream. Nonetheless, the principle by which *Paterson* would move within each facet-plane and from facet-plane to facet-plane was established: it would be coincidence. Pun, ambiguity, and the selection of key words, bidirectional actions and images would emphasize similarity and contrast in a way different from his earlier simultaneist experiments. At one time Williams even considered including Lyle among the work's authors, but changed his mind. In his review of *Paterson I* (1946), Randall Jarrell points out how the double exclamations of "clearly" and "divorce" are used to suggest pattern, and Joel Conarroe's *William Carlos Williams' 'Paterson': Language and Landscape* (1970) argues for the poem's organization and unity based upon these patterns.

Williams' expression of gratitude to Nash for his "discovery" may have been provoked by Jarrell's later attitude toward the poem, which increasingly began to dismiss its unity and use of prose as capricious. His "A View of Three Poets" (1951) states finally: "It is interesting to see how much some later parts of *Paterson* resemble in their structure some middle and later parts of the *Cantos:* the Organization of Irrelevance (or, perhaps, the Irrelevance of Organization) suggests itself as a name for this category of structure. Such organization is *ex post facto* organization: if something is somewhere, one can always find Some Good Reason for its being there, but if it had not been there would one reader have missed it? If it had been put somewhere else, would one reader have guessed where it should have 'really' gone?" [29] Striking close to the poem's "uncoded" source, Jarrell concludes that Chance is "sole arbiter" of the work. Even Robert Lowell, who praises *Paterson II* in the *Nation* (1948), is compelled to refer to its "chunks of prose" as "raw" though, in an especially apt comparison, he senses a kinship of the approach to the use of factual material in the didactic chapters of Herman Melville's *Moby-Dick*. Both poets, however, proceed from a concept of unity in an art work which, like the concept of unity in easel pictures, was being tested and supplanted. Greenberg's "The Crisis of the Easel Picture" (1948) notes of the revolution: "The easel picture subordinates decorative to dramatic effect. It cuts the illusion of a box-like cavity into the wall behind it, and within this, as a unity, it organizes three-dimensional semblances. To the extent that the artist flattens out the cavity for the sake of decorative patterning and organizes its contents in terms of flatness and frontality, the essence of the easel picture—which is not the same as its quality—is on the way to being compromised." [30] The very building out of synthetic cubism requires a new kind of expectation on the part of the viewer and hence a new kind of unity.

Although Williams disagreed generally with T. S. Eliot, his statement about needing to remake himself seems close to Eliot's statement on Shakespeare in "John Ford" (1932): "The whole of Shakespeare's work is *one* poem. . . . A man might, hypothetically, compose any number of fine passages or even of whole poems which would each give satisfaction, and yet not be a great poet, unless we felt them to be united by one significant, consistent, and developing personality." [31] For Williams, who appends John Addington Symonds' elucidation of the practice of Hipponax to the opening book of the poem, the unity of *Paterson* might lie in its integration with his own personality, as in his earlier poems the recurrent myth of Kora had suggested that those descents and returns were related to a psychological need "to gather the assets of the whole personality together" into the form of a personified thought at moments of despair and spatial closure "and with this united strength to fling open the door of the future." Indicating that the presence of Book V is a denial of the internal unity of *Paterson*'s first four books, Walter Sutton in "Dr. Williams' *Paterson* and the Quest for Form" (1960) comes to a like position: "The search for form and the quest for identity are the same. Neither the city, the poet, nor the poem is a self-sufficient entity. They are interdependent elements of a cultural complex, and the definition of any one involves interaction." [32] Sutton cites in support Williams' statement in *I Wanted to Write a Poem* that *Paterson V* is needed not because he feels some organic lack but because *he* no longer believes that death ends anything. But Sutton might also have cited the lines in Book III of *Paterson* where Williams speaks paradoxically of the clarity of the blurring "between man and / his writing" so one is no longer certain "as to which is the man and / which the thing and of them both which / is the more to be valued" (P, 140).

One suspects that the surprise which Williams expresses at Nash's "*ex post facto* organization" comes precisely because he was uneasy about this avenue of a unity within as a possible approach to the work. Indication of this is provided in his letter to Norman Macleod (1945). Fearing that *Paterson* might not be accepted "because of its formlessness," Williams had written: "Christ! Are there no intelligent men left in the world? Dewey might do something for me, but I am not worth his notice" (SL, 239). The reference is undoubtedly to John Dewey's extension of the Jamesian "stream of consciousness" into "contexts of experience." These "contexts" saw the continuity of life as a gradation of qualitative fusions, here and there broken into by articulated analyses and discriminations. Unity in art became a system of fusions, including those with "fringe" elements outside the art work, a system that existed so long as a problematic situation did not arise to force breakage by a discontinuous counter quality of discrimination or analysis. When Nash was able to find counterpoint in the work, Williams could feel more at ease that such a dominant quality of fusion did occur and that his new poetics did not "destroy" the "unity" of the old, much in the same way he could feel at ease with controlled measure, having felt, as his "An Essay on *Leaves of Grass*" (1955) notes, that free verse was immoral.

The new poetics, as Greenberg was to relate it in art, had much to do with altering illusion: "This tendency appears in the all-over, 'decentralized,' 'polyphonic' picture that relies on a surface knit together of identical or closely similar elements which repeat themselves without marked variation from one edge of the picture to the other. It is a kind of picture that dispenses, apparently, with beginning, middle, end. Though the 'all-over' picture will, when successful, still hang dramatically on a wall, it comes very close to decoration—to the kind seen in wallpaper patterns that can be repeated indefinitely—and insofar as the 'all-over' picture remains an easel picture, which somehow it does, it infects the notion of the genre with a fatal ambiguity."[33] The music terminology, Greenberg confesses, was borrowed advisedly from the work Kurt List and René Leibowitz had done on Schönberg's methods of composition, especially in light of Kahnweiler's earlier equating of Gris's form of cubism and Schönberg's twelve-tone music.

Critics have been quick to note the musical basis of the repetitive devices in *Paterson,* but in so doing, they have slighted the work's connection with painting. Jarrell, for example, in "The Poet and His Public" (1946) calls "the organization of *Paterson* . . . musical to an almost unprecedented degree: Dr. Williams introduces a theme that stands for an idea, repeats it over and over in varied forms, develops it side by side with two or three more themes that are being developed, recurs to it time and time again throughout the poem, and echoes it for ironic or grotesque effects in thoroughly incongruous contexts." [34] Thomas R. Whitaker in *William Carlos Williams* (1968) goes so far as to deny the metaphor of painting: "In trying to elucidate . . . we may be tempted to discuss the poem as a mosaic or as some other spatial form. But to do so would be to lose sight of its temporal core. And even a musical analogy, which may enable us to talk about its orchestration of themes, cannot fully cope with its existential mode of progression." [35] Greenberg concludes his discussion of the crisis of the easel picture by returning, like Williams, to personality as the final arbiter of structure: "The dissolution of the pictorial into sheer texture, into apparently sheer sensation, into an accumulation of repetitions, seems to speak for and answer something profound in contemporary sensibility." [36]

But none of these issues resolves finally the issues of dimensionality in *Paterson*, though they provide a feasible basis for one's discussion of it. The dimensionality of synthetic cubism which does intrude on actual life space is still different from the dimensionality of a poem which, however modified, remains a system of illusions, none of which in the end leaves the actual dimensions of the printed page. Thus the intrusion of art into the life space of the reader is, in effect, a psychological intrusion predicated upon a separation which is made mentally between fact and fiction, individual and poem, and it is this separation that Williams is attacking. For him, as he reiterated time and again, both art and nature are parts of the one cyclical process of descent and return, and through both one may live more fully. Previously he had kept the two separate enough so that nature might be illuminated by art and art by nature. Book I of *Paterson,* which opens with a colon and closes with a statement about the interrelatedness of art and life, ends this clear separation. The colon usually indicates that what follows is an explanation, a list, an enumeration connected to what has preceded. Here what has preceded is clearly nature, and thus, from the very onset, with the statement of the poem's *"plan for action to supplant a plan for action"* to the book's end, in an espousal of what Yvor Winters would call "the fallacy of imitative form," an assault on a separation of art and nature occurs. Within this larger assault lie the smaller battles of factual and fictional art, male and female, past and present, one and many, and marriage and divorce.

The assault, which begins so forthrightly with the "plan for action" and the concluding epigraph from Symonds, blurs by the middle of the work as the poet begins a withdrawal from Dr. Paterson that makes his own presence in the poem less intrusive. The withdrawal works against some of the close continuities between individual and poem and life and art space which the techniques of synthetic cubism and his earlier statements suggest he might be resolving. Part of the withdrawal is necessary, for, as Sherman Paul's *The Music of Survival* (1968) rightly maintains, "The poet who has made the poem has not failed in the way the poet in the poem has: Williams has been able to take up the materials of his particular place and make a poem of them, and he must be granted some recognition as a poet of his culture." [37] Williams' very ability to arrange these smaller battles within the work's overriding themes of divorce and blockage is different from Paterson's frustrated wanderings. Taking place in facet-planes whose "interpenetration [is] both ways," the battles are intended to result within the work in rest. Hopefully they will form the "picture of perfect rest" defined by the poet in *Kora* as the basis of permanence in art, and, as characterized by his Objectivist poetics, their bidirectional stresses will lie open not to the psychological descents and returns of the early poetry and cubism but to a contrary illusion of eternality. As one cannot progress in and out of blockage, the "hopeless and desperate situations" which these facet-planes contain and which earlier had moved the poet from life into art and then back into life or from present into past and then back into present, become, in his abandonment of extrastructural devices for conveying authorial presence and interference, merely decorative.

As this authorial interference diminishes, the reader increasingly encounters the mechanical coherence of the work's machined contours and ornamentally raw prose segments and heraldic, suspended clusters of signs and lyrics. These compose the theater of illusion for which he is to suspend willingly his disbelief and, by the work's close, he is more willing to admit a designer's surface than a poet's craft. Defined by sequence, spatial metaphors, parallelism, and repetition, the lateral movements may reveal the intrinsic relationships of the parts, but the reader cannot say that he has rescued anything "human" from their arrangement. The thematic descent into hell which occurs in Book III does not, like the ends of Books I and II, return the reader to life. Nor does the image of death which ends Book IV and from which the young poet and the swimmer spring in a new beginning so much conclude the work as confirm its preoccupation with continuity, suggested by its title Pater-son and the closing image of the hanged John John-son.

This continuity, as Williams' "Letter to an Australian Editor" (1946) reveals, may represent yet another discrepancy between poet and protagonist, intent and realization. The continuity was not conceived originally as male to male. It was supposed to reside not in "the assumption that it was mind that fertilizes mind" and in a cutting of one's self "from that supplying female" (society), but in a renewal of "the close tie between the poet and the upsurging (or down surging) forms of his immediate world." [88] In short, it was to reside, as Williams later told Edith Heal, in a view of language not as communication but as action, as productive of art. Unlike "A Coronal," whose initial prophecy of spring is carried operatively and thematically into its conclusion, Book IV, which may bring the reader operatively into the presence of art, leaves him thematically not in some inexorable natural process but in a rhetoric of futurity. This rhetoric is the "reality" from which the protagonist tries to escape at the close of Book III and which like the dog of Book II must somehow be combed out. Book III had warned that "the future is no answer" (P, 173), and Book V, realizing the error of the poet's earlier conclusion, reiterates, "Not prophecy! NOT prophecy! / but the thing itself!" (P, 242).

Such futurity may well be the price of the work's blurring nature and art. Where else but in the future can the poem be resolved since, unless one is willing to concede its existence as a second level of interpretation, its own inner processes eliminate the present and the past as possibilities? One might even be willing to argue that futurity becomes a problem only because the poem as process takes on so much reality that the poet no doubt felt that it had achieved what it needed within the illusions created by its structure. He had no further need for extrastructural devices like those he used in Books I–III. By analogy to painting, this would mean that he had reverted to the devices of a frame and a two-dimensional canvas after having suggested in one part of his work that affixing materials offered the only answer to its problems of dimensionality and organization, thereby making implicit what had been explicit. Or one might argue that the act of art which becomes the theme of *Paterson V* is already implicit in Books I–IV and that the poet makes it explicit only because his readers had been so caught up in what the poem was saying that they had not understood what it was doing. Yet the very shift from doing to saying conveys something about the limitations of the first four books. Despite a descent into hell, their failure to maintain extrastructural devices or to move back into an immediate world within their own structure prevents any psychological affirmations like those which resolve the early poems. Their totality projects an analytic answer to what at the start was clearly an impulse to a synthetic mode.

In "William Carlos Williams' *Paterson*" (1965), Richard Gustafson proposes that the repetitions are designed to "show the various ways by which man tries to unlock his mind to find beauty" [39]—dead history, self-indulgence, books, the future, and finally art; but, whereas one might concede that these themes, like their corresponding metaphors of man (the Passaic Falls), woman (the park), artificial man (the city), and artificial woman (society), are phenomenologically right in their outward movement, they are mechanical in that except for imagination, that "hole / in the bottom of the bag" (P, 247) which he describes in *Paterson V,* the blockage which the poet depicts prevents any smooth outward flow. Yet a poem about blockage whose operative mode conveys facility would defeat the theme, just as a semanticist's 300-page manuscript about man's inability to communicate defeats by an underlying hope of communication its own basic premise. One feels that the poet would have been wiser to center his poem on the theme of difficult passage rather than on that of blockage, and studies like Walter Scott Peterson's *An Approach to 'Paterson'* (1967), which argue for the poem's success, take precisely this line. Nevertheless, one should not assume that the failure of the work's overall design to merge seamlessly with its content totally defeats it as a significant production or precludes the successes of many of its parts. As in much Romantic poetry, the "failed" long poem becomes the vehicle for a series of small lyrical successes, and often in the work's course, the reader comes across powerful and exquisite sections. In some instances such as the Beautiful Thing episode of Book III, these lyrics had been written long before their inclusion in the poem; but in others such as the protagonist's reminiscences of trips to the Solarium, the hospital, and the movies with his son, they appear new and provide some preview of the poet's eventual direction in "Asphodel, That Greeny Flower" (1954).

Nor should one let the failures of dimensionality and descent obscure the poem's conscious and innovative use of cubism. Like Gris, who proposed to move from cylinders to particular bottles, Williams announces early in Book I that he will move "from mathematics to particulars," and a structural principle of facet-planes constructed like those of "To a Solitary Disciple," by breaks and parallelism, is clear. Moreover, whatever the technique may owe to others, the warp and woof which the poet identifies as a second characteristic of cubism are clearly these particulars being played against the image of the falls. As Sister Bernetta Quinn indicates in *"Paterson:* Listening to Landscape" (1970), Williams in one tentative beginning encircled with heavy blue crayon the sentence: "It is the FALLS, continuously falling; use it as background to everything else, to heighten everything else and to stitch together every other thing." [40] He also marked the passage at the side with red crayon. The plan which the poet summarized for readers when Book IV appeared (1949) reaffirmed this intention: "From the beginning I decided there would be four books following the course of the river whose life seemed more and more to resemble my own life as I more and more thought of it: the river above the Falls, the catastrophe of the Falls itself, the river below the Falls, and the entrance at the end into the great sea." [41]

Various critics have spotted the connection of this river with the mind's stream of consciousness, making this concept of the flow of thought ultimately the source of the abstract, architectural strands with which the individual lines will interlace. Support for their identification may be found both within *Paterson* and in "The Mind Hesitant" (1948), where the poet admits, "Sometimes the river / becomes a river in the mind / or of the mind / or in and of the mind" (CLP, 118). The connection already prefigures the emphasis on memory which "Asphodel" will assume as its tie with the past. Earlier, in "The Poet of *Paterson Book One"* (1946), Tyler had suggested the river's connection with the Liffey and James Joyce's *Finnegans Wake,* and Sister Bernetta Quinn in her essay offers another connection with the Don and Mikhail Sholokhov's *And Quiet Flows the Don.* But an even more proximate source is the poet's description of the Arno in *A Voyage to Pagany.* There he calls the river "the prototype of art," and goes on ecstatically to proclaim: "Useless river—as far as itself is concerned. Gathers dewdrops from flower petals just the same. Carries them just the same. Nobody gives a damn. Goes under the old bridge. The prototype of art just the same." Then, realizing it has a Florence of its own, he addresses the flow as a kind of lusty, mirror, ideal poet: "Arno! maker. . . . You must begin with nothing, like a river in the morning and make, make new. Arno! I want you to say this, I want you to take me into Florence from upstream and that is all I want you to say. . . . The Arno, forever recreating its own loveliness" (VP, 48).

In addition, a cubist solidification of language is apparent in the poet's going out into life and introducing "life" language into "literary" language. This solidification lies behind the poet's using letters, newspaper accounts, documents, histories, advertisements, dialogue, an interview, an engineer's report, epigraphs, and other clearly nonillustrious aids to strengthen the illusion that art and nature are intermingling. The very typography with its differently sized fonts for prose and poetry, its inventive use of periods, its approximation of signs and commands as well as of its own intrastructural collage (P, 164) conveys much of the plasticity that is meant also to inhere in meaning. The solidification is supported, too, by the belief noted in the *Autobiography* that, "in the very lay of the syllables

Paterson," he intended not God but a locus to be discovered (A, 392). Thus, whatever he may have owed to Lyle for suggesting the breakthrough which permitted him to use many of these items, Williams was right in thinking that his alterations of his source were such as to make the nature of these items different from, though not necessarily antagonistic to, Lyle's purposes. The very emphasis on thought as stream of consciousness reflected in the grounding image of the falls rather than as the "coded" category that Lyle's system of indentations would have produced keeps him from the abstractions that he consistently associates with knowledge gone wrong.

What the failures of dimensionality and descent do suggest then about *Paterson* and its attempts to use cubism is a confirmation of Pound's feelings in "Dr. Williams' Position" (1928) that if Williams ever used form he would use it ab exteriore and that when "plot, major form, or outline" are "put on ab exteriore, they probably lead only to dullness, confusion or remplissage or the 'falling between two stools' " (WCW, 35). Perhaps until one is willing to accept a literature whose structure is even far more radical than that of *Paterson,* the techniques of synthetic cubism will never successfully translate into those of poetry. Nevertheless, their use in the design of *Paterson* clearly removes the poem from the immediacy and urgency of Williams' lyrics and, as clearly, signals the critic to treat its elements differently. At best, the poem is, as Roy Harvey Pearce's *The Continuity of American Poetry* (1961) suggests, a lyric-epic. As a lyric-epic it uses the platform space created at the expense of synthetic cubism by its own prophecy as a locus from which to observe the present conforming to a prescribed plan. The voyeurism which this vantage point makes possible, different in kind from that suggested in the *Autobiography* by Williams' observation of patients, provides the psychic distance which Joyce's *A Portrait of the Artist as a Young Man* (1916) makes requisite to one's writing in the epical form. This platform space, by its tendency to separate, provides Williams a center of an emotional gravity that is equidistant from him and from others, but without the prolonged brooding upon himself that Joyce defines as the method of the poet's achieving such distancing.

Williams' lyrics, which like Joyce's definition of the form were predicated upon the "simplest verbal vesture of an instant of emotion," by their very nature resisted a structure, even prophecy, imposed from the outside. These early poems as a consequence carry in their realizations clear unconscious patterns, and one feels that these unconscious patterns provide them in part with their strength. When Williams uses conscious patterns as he does in *Paterson* and even to a degree in "Asphodel," one cannot help feeling that despite certain gains in range and subject there occurs, too, a lessening or diverting of his strength. In addition, the link with his earlier works that Williams wishes to forge by using these conscious patterns and, in *Paterson,* by extending his tendencies toward art resists by a very outwardness a knowledge and close-knit summation of experience toward which both his personal and professional lives seemed at this time inclined. As early as 1932 he had written Hartley, "I look forward to twenty years of continued development . . . with time for summations and reminiscences after that" (SL, 122), and, as early as the third section of *Paterson II* (1948), one can see that these summations and reminiscences had begun.

CHAPTER THREE

"Asphodel": The Dream Recalled

꙳   When William Carlos Williams recovered from the
cerebral attacks which had occurred in 1951 and 1952, he
began writing again. "My whole interest in poetry," he
notes in *I Wanted to Write a Poem* (1958), "now was in
developing the concept I had discovered—the variable
foot" (IWWP, 88–89). The development which his Introduction to Byron Vazakas' *Transfigured Night* (1946)
shows him already verging on could allow him to put an
end to his lifelong insecurity about "controlled measure"
and permit him the confidence evident in his final works.
In his essay on *Leaves of Grass* (1955), this confidence
enables him as well to attack T. S. Eliot for his failure to
come up with something equally significant in his return
of poetic technique to the academy: "Not that he [Eliot]
didn't in his verse try it on, for size, let us say, in his later
experiments, particularly in *Four Quartets,* but even there
he soon came to the end of his rope. The accented strophe
he had definitely given up, . . . but to infer from that fact
that he discovered the freedom of a new measure was not
true. It looked to me, at least, as if there were some pro-

found depth to his probing beyond which he dared not go without compromising his religious faith. He did not attempt it" (ELG, 25). Still, John C. Thirlwall's "Ten Years of a New Rhythm" (1962) reports that "Williams found that this form, even when measured, could not completely express the modern idiom." "There was the danger," he reveals, "that even with the 'variable foot,' the triadic stanza might become monotonous as free verse had become monotonous" (PB, 183).

Despite his earlier use of tripart structures, the very threeness of the measure would by its number impose upon Williams certain thematic limitations. Besides an early reference to "the rule of three" as being "mystical" and having forced its inventors to formulate mathematics, other reservations to the number appear in "Against the Weather" (1939): "Dante was a craftsman of supreme skill, his emphasis upon a triple unity is an emphasis upon structure. All his elements are in three. In the solid structure of the Spaniard [Juan Ruiz, the author of *Libro de buen amor*], far less skilfully made, it is important to note the flat-footed quadruple rhyme scheme as opposed to the unfinished three of the Italian dogmatist. The emphasis is on structure, the sensual structure of the verse" (SE, 206). "Note that beginning with the first line of the *terza rima* at any given onset," Williams continues, showing that Dante, the poet, triumphs over Dante, the dogmatist, "every four lines following contain a dissonance. . . . Throughout the *Commedia* this fourth unrhymed factor, unobserved, is the entrance of Pan to the Trinity which restores it to the candid embrace of love underlying the peculiar, faulty love of the great poem which makes remote, by virtue, that which possessed, illuminates the

Spanish epic" (SE, 207). A letter to Henry Wells (1955) registers the same complaint against the number: "Shifting at once, to save time, the trinity always seemed unstable. It lacked a fourth member, the devil. I found myself always conceiving my abstract designs as possessing four sides. That was natural enough with spring, summer, autumn and winter always before me. To leave any one of them out would have been unthinkable" (SL, 333).

Besides suggesting the very revealing equation of the number four with flesh, the world, and the devil, these statements make clear the inherently "nonmaterial" bias of the triadic structure. This nonmaterialness would be bound to disturb anyone who in his youthful dreams had been as committed as Williams was to verifying poetry in nature and whose structural use of four was apparent at least as early as the italicized improvisations of *Kora in Hell* (1920). Since the conscious discovery of the line coincided with a recovery from a cerebral attack, there is some reason to connect the two. As Williams' nervous excitement had contributed to the line length of his poetry, the new line may well have been devised to compensate for the physical effects of the strokes which made it difficult for the poet to return his gaze quickly to the left margin of a page. The staggered margins of the triadic line were almost imperative as a corrective. Conjointly, since the poet was forced to rely upon memory and secondhand information during the illness, there may have seemed no need to add a fourth element—direct observation—to the line. Of lesser significance may have been the belief that were he to decide on four as his root number he might convey to others an added, unwanted indebtedness to Vazakas' previous use of a four line structure. Moreover, if one attributes the use of the line to the strokes, one can understand, too, why, as Williams recovered from their effects and needed the staggered margins less and could rely more upon direct observation, he would grow impatient with the measure. By 1955, he could already embark on a strenuous reading tour of colleges across the nation, and his dependence upon the triadic line does cease about the same time that he begins circulating again in these public readings. That, in assembling his early essays for *Selected Essays* (1954), he may also have been moved to return to earlier beliefs about the life value of poetry may be a real and added factor in the measure's demise.

Nevertheless, the discovery of the new variable foot could permit him the immediate realization of two other dreams. His essay on *Leaves of Grass* explains that it would allow him, first, to make his discovery of a new line as Columbus had made his discovery of a New World within a nontranscendental context: "Man finds himself on earth whether he likes it or not, with nowhere else to go. What then is to become of him? Obviously we can't stand still or we shall be destroyed. Then if there is no room for us on the outside we shall, in spite of ourselves, have to go *in:* into the cell, the atom, the poetic line, for our discoveries. We have to break the old apart to make room for ourselves, whatever may be our tragedy and however we may fear it" (ELG, 31). Next, by virtue of its inward thrust, the verse technique could complement his lifetime effort to know life by being able to represent more accurately thought processes. As the *Autobiography* (1951) affirms in regard to Gertrude Stein, a writer's knowledge "concerns the whole man," and includes both psychic and somatic factors. Williams' Imagist period which had stressed the somatic at the expense of the psychic had not, in its effort to copy the rhythms of the body, tried to use the concepts of stream of consciousness on which both Gertrude Stein and James Joyce had built their works or the discoveries of Sigmund Freud which had progressively gained wider acceptance in life and literature after World War I. This stream of consciousness which makes the uninterrupted, uneven, and endless expression of consciousness the form of art could, by its very negation of an imposed outline different from experience, end the necessity for the decorative, abstract bones of a structure imposed upon experience to give it meaning.

Consistent with these concepts and discoveries, the techniques in these poems written after Williams' attacks show an emphasis on memory, whose "movements / are towards new objectives / (even though formerly they were abandoned)" (P, 96). As such, the emphasis offers insight into the nature of the new mental process that becomes a logical extension of Objectivism's stress on intrinsic form as well as into the new way the Kora myth would function in the poet's work. Whereas formerly the psychic descents produced by the "hopeless and desperate situations" moved the writer from life into art and then back into life, now the autotelic descents would move him from the present to the past, here represented by past art works, and then back into the present. The "wisdom" that the descents would rescue comes in their revival of the "abandoned movements" of youthful dreams. The essay on Charles Henri Ford (1939) makes these revivals integral to the phenomenal world of a writer's later years if he is to be rated "a master." Thus, Williams' views of his own artistic life circles back upon himself in a manner where the expression of consciousness becomes the form and, in mirror of poems like "The Wanderer," the young Williams stands as the rescuing double of the infirm, older poet.

"Asphodel," because of the reentrance of the Kora myth, however much the myth is altered, contrasts markedly with the poetry of Williams' Objectivist period where the relationships of the objects sung resided in an eternal present. This eternal present was formed, as his experiments in simultaneism suggest, by equating language with color or, as the essay on Marianne Moore (1925) explains, by the intersection of lines to establish points. This intersection, like the intersection of planes in cubist and post-cubist art, alters the perspective upon which the illusion of depth depends. The flattened planes which result create an illusion of tension which, in turn, casts light upon the intent of Williams' particular choice of sky, red, yellow, and green, as the evocative blocks of "Silence" (1944): "He [the poet] might carry it [the intersection of loci] further and say in his imagination that apprehension perforates at places, through to understanding—as white is at the intersection of blue and green and yellow and red. It is this white light that is the background of all good work" (SE, 122). This "white light" expands Williams' assertion in "The Great Sex Spiral" (1917) that truth lies at the intersection of loci into an Objectivist approximation of the "picture of perfect rest" mentioned in the Imagist *Kora* as occurring when two contending forces are equal. In this approximation, the Imagist tension between control (ego, light) and variability (id, dark) joins a second, new tension between past and present to bring about the stasis.

In as much as Williams wanted the structures in which

he would present this stasis to be consistent with contemporary notions of thought processes, he was correct in assuming that for his depiction both the iambic pentameter which he had long rejected and free verse which he abandoned in 1924 were inappropriate. What he would call "the Shakespearean form" goes back to a representation of the mind's working that is older than stream of consciousness or Freud. It derives from a time when the mind was thought to consist of compartments (loci), each of which could contain in isolation a topos, or controlling image, about which certain experiences would cluster along systems of comparison, contrast, contiguity, and cause-and-effect. Each compartment, moreover, was separated from other loci and their accretions. The system antedates scientific notions of brain functions and represents the interiorization of artificial memory house techniques, already fully formed in prehistoric times. In these techniques, which were allied early to lyric poetry, objects were committed to memory by locating them in rooms (stanze), and the word still obtains in the divisions (compartments) of a poem. Likewise, the pentameter line, which in English usually breaks when spoken into halves, ideally conforms to a system of Western thought based upon balance, comparison, proportion, contrast, cause-and-effect, and the viewing of things dually. It is not very consistent with the imbalance, pluralism, and dynamism which, following the pragmatists, Williams felt compelled to stress. Reviewing Wallace Stevens' *The Man with the Blue Guitar* for *The New Republic,* he gives evidence as early as 1937 of having dealt with some of these concerns: "Five beats to the line here [in "Owl's Clover"], and that's where the trouble is let in. These five beats have a strange effect on a modern poet; they make him think he wants to think." [1]

With the elimination of the line-halving caesura and of superimposed proportion, something still possible with Vazakas' discovery, free verse was somewhat better at avoiding the dichotomies inherent in the structure of the pentameter line and in the exact compartmentalization of the stanza. Nonetheless, without a controlling inner force, it, too, proved extremely limited. In the hands of Williams, its stress on the somatic and its lack of projection for building poems let it easily run down, having, as he remarked, "no formal necessity implicit in it." For, if poetry were to relate to a future, as he now wanted it to do, it must set up a structure that extends into futurity rather than one that simply reacts by looking back toward experience. He realized that, to avoid falling into Absolutism, he would have to permit this structure and sense of futurity—not prophecy but the setting up of fixed relationships within the relative field of a work of art similar to the fixed relationship of light to the relative, moving universe that Albert Einstein had outlined. Now, controlled by a triadic line (ego), which by insisting on two caesuras enormously enlarges the flexibility of the single-caesura line, and utilizing a "variable foot" (id), the poem could achieve all the relativism of free verse, plus order.

Still, whether because of the strokes or because of a new emphasis on mind, Williams could not achieve this stress on relativism without some loss of vividness. "The Orchestra" (1952) announces that "It is not / a flute note either, it is the relation / of the flute note / to a drum" (PB, 81) that the poet seeks. This loss can best be gauged in the differing effects of the almost diagnostic care for detail in a poem like "The Red Wheelbarrow" (1923) and the more generically described details of the poems in *The Desert Music and Other Poems* (1954) and *Journey to Love* (1955). "The Red Wheelbarrow" ideally instances the stability that "Notes from a Talk on Poetry" (1919) likens to Villon's frozen ink pot at the conclusion of the *Petit Testament*. Its objects have become symbols of man by their having crystallized emotions into facts. "Seventy Years Deep" (1954) explains the origin of the poem as "affection for an old Negro named Marshall. He had been a fisherman, caught porgies off Gloucester. He used to tell me how he had to work in the hold in freezing weather, standing ankle deep in cracked ice packing down the fish. He said he didn't feel cold. He never felt cold in his life until just recently. I liked that man, and his son Milton almost as much. In his back yard I saw the red wheelbarrow surrounded by the white chickens." Williams supposes that his "affection for the old man somehow got into the writing" [2] of the poem.

In the course of the work the almost precisionist feel for objects details how rain "glazes" the wheelbarrow, converting it into a figurine or a pot like that jar which Stevens' "Anecdote of the Jar" (1919) had placed in Tennessee and about which a "slovenly wilderness"—like Williams' white chickens—took its meaning. Indeed, ignoring the poet's description of the work's origin, many readers have made the poem a Stevensian exercise, connecting the meaning of its opening lines—"so much depends / upon"—to the poet or the poem's objects rather than to the survival of Marshall and his family. Roy Harvey Pearce's *The Continuity of American Poetry* (1961) offers the fullest state-

ment of their position: "In this notably sentimental piece
. . . Williams can only dimly specify 'what' depends—
himself in his vocation as poet. He assures himself that he
is what he is by virtue of his power to collate such objects
into sharply annotated images like these. He must feel
himself into the things of his world; for he is dependent
on them as occasions to be himself, as poet. Perhaps—and
herein lies the pathos—they depend on him as much as he
depends on them. 'So much depends' too upon a poet's
being there to make them what, at their best, they can be:
objects in a poem" (WCW, 97).

Within the painterly bias of *The Hieroglyphics of a New
Speech* (1969), Bram Dijkstra repeats Pearce's reading:
"The poem is a perfect representation of . . . a moment,
caught at the point of its highest visual significance, in perfectly straightforward, 'realistic,' but highly selective detail; each word has its intrinsic evocative function, focusing the object and its essential structural relationship to
its immediate surroundings in concrete terms. . . . Because the artist has focused on the object under these particular circumstances, has *seen* the relationship it bears to
his own position within the objective world, his statement
of fact comes to represent his own feeling as well." [3] Less
complex and more obviously in keeping with the meaning
of the Stevens poem, Neil Myers' "William Carlos Williams' *Spring and All*" (1965) reduces the work's emphasis
to the objects alone: "In the famous, extremely reduced
'Red Wheelbarrow,' an inconspicuous scene is brought to
expression by focusing on relationships: on the barrow
'glazed with rain / water,' asserting itself at the heart of the
scene and pulling everything together; and on an outright
introductory statement of significance, 'so much depends,'

which, in view of the trivial objects, barrow and chickens, seems firmly impertinent." [4]

More important, critics have stressed the poem's vividness as its method of redeeming its subject. James E. Breslin's *William Carlos Williams* (1970) asks: "How can a poem about things as hopelessly ordinary as a wheelbarrow and white chickens be anything but flat?" His answer is that "Williams risks banality in order to push through to startling discoveries. The scene is not entirely bare: the wheelbarrow is red and it has just been rained on, giving it a fresh, 'glazed' appearance. A spare, clinical manner, it is clear, asserts by relief the primary color and novelty that are there. We are brought down, into a new world." [5] Earlier, Alan Ostrom's *The Poetic World of William Carlos Williams* (1966) had noted: "Here, as so often in his poems, the excitement and vision of reality derive from Williams' using as the typical object central to his order an object that the reader would not have thought representative of the qualities that Williams finds in it. This disparity between the conventionally assigned values (actuality) and those newly discovered as reality performs the same function as the bringing together of apparently unrelated things in conventional metaphor: it provides a fresh view of reality in the perception of the previously unseen relationship." [6]

In "A Negro Woman" (1955) and poems like it, the exact reversal of this process occurs; rather than an emotion's having been frozen into a fact, man has become the symbol of something close to an emotion: of memory, possibly, since the woman's marigolds are "wrapped / in an old newspaper"; of art, perhaps, since the flowers approximate the sheaf of grain that versions of the Kora myth show Demeter bearing; but in either case, of "another world" as the poem concedes (PB, 123). This "other world," the final image of the flowers as a torch suggests, may even be physical, for the torch makes the woman carrying the marigolds a black Statue of Liberty. Despite these differences, she functions as had the wheelbarrow as an object to order the poem's other parts. Yet, whereas critics have argued that vividness redeemed the banalities of "The Red Wheelbarrow," here one must argue for suggestiveness. Only one word—"torch"—shows any power to bring the situation to life. The other details are kept vague. The marigolds are a "bunch," their wrapping is an "old newspaper," they are "pretty," and "of two shades." The woman is reduced to being "bareheaded," her thighs a "bulk" that causes "her to waddle." The window she passes, like the streets later, go undescribed. Williams is no longer the physician who in the midst of epidemics is able to remark that medicine "sharpened the sight . . . , the extraneous is everything that is not seen in detail. There is no time not to notice" (I, 273). Indeed, in his shift to imagination and memory, what he recognizes as extraneous is the crystallized fact, and it seems for the present that he is willing to let such recognitions stand. An intermediary stage in this reversal may well be the figures of Sam Patch and Mrs. Cumming in *Paterson I* (1946). Here, either as "a body found next spring / frozen in an ice-cake" (Patch) or as "a body / fished next day from the muddy swirl" (Mrs. Cumming), each had become the frozen fact of emotion, associated in turn by Williams with the vaguer emotions surrounding their inabilities to communicate (P, 31). The effect is underscored by Patch's particular encasement.

88

Still, if the poems of the late volumes represent a loss of vividness, the order implicit in the threeness of their triadic lines can permit Williams to enter the more overtly moral poetry of his final years. In *The Desert Music and Other Poems,* the first of the books to be written after his strokes, a poem for his daughters-in-law, "To Daphne and Virginia" (1953), asserts: "The mind is the cause of our distresses / but of it we can build anew" (PB, 73). "The Orchestra" makes this building imperative: "Man has survived hitherto because he was too ignorant to know how to realize his wishes. Now that he can realize them, he must either change them or perish" (PB, 82). "For Eleanor and Bill Monahan" (1953) wishes explorers to direct "their ships" inward and "To a Dog Injured in the Street" (1953) equates René Char's belief "in the power of beauty / to right all wrong" (PB, 88) with Williams' own. Thus, during a period of American United Nations action in Korea and of long public discussions on the moral effects of atomic bombing, to offset the death-wish (destruction) of science and the equally destructive "misty escapism" of religion, Williams embraces a position for poetry close to that which Matthew Arnold's "The Study of Poetry" (1880) had propounded: "The future of poetry is immense, because in poetry, where it is worthy of its high destinies, our race, as time goes on, will find an ever surer and surer stay. There is not a creed which is not shaken, not an accredited dogma which is not shown to be questionable, not a received tradition which does not threaten to dissolve. Our religion has materialized itself in the fact, in the supposed fact; it has attached its emotion to the fact, and now the fact is failing it. But for poetry the idea is everything; the rest is a world of illusion, of divine illusion. Poetry attaches its emotion to the idea; the idea *is* the fact. The strongest part of our religion to-day is its unconscious poetry." [7]

The position is, in addition, an extension of the stand taken in "Against the Weather": "But the artist . . . can never be a liar. He has to perpetuate his trust on an unlying scale. If he fails, the character of his failure lies precisely there, his crime, for which I condemn him to the eighth circle of hell, dry rot. Of all moral hells that of the faithless artist is the worst since his responsibility is the greatest" (SE, 211–212). For Williams the trust consists in the artist's believing in and building toward a better future. Still, this moral position which Williams assumes is not a moralistic one. As he remarks in *I Wanted to Write a Poem* of Randall Jarrell's inability to "take the identification of the filthy river with the perversion of the characters" in Book IV of *Paterson:* "If you are going to write realistically of the conception of filth in the world, it can't be pretty. . . . With the approach to the city, international character began to enter the innocent river and pervert it; sexual perversions, such things that every metropolis when you get to know it houses. . . . When human beings herd together, have to face each other, they are likely to go crooked. What in the world is an artist to do? He is not a moralist. He *sees* things, reacts to them, must take them into consideration. . . . I had to take the characters and show them graphically" (IWWP, 79).

Furthermore, for Williams the need for control (ego) had at this time a second cause, his growing sense that the descent, which represents life's dying into art, must be stated in terms of that death. Consonant with the alterations in the Kora myth, the "art" herein represents the dreams of youth as realized in early poems as well as memories of past forms of art works not by Williams. His explanation of the purpose of Book V of *Paterson* in *I Wanted to Write a Poem* clearly indicates this: *"Paterson V* must be written, is being written, and the gulls [of "Gulls"] appear at the beginning. Why must it be written? *Paterson IV* ends with the protagonist breaking through the bushes, identifying himself with the land, with America. He really will die but it can't be categorically stated that death ends *anything*. When you're through with sex, with ambition, what can an old man create? Art, of course, a piece of art that will go beyond him into the lives of young people, the people who haven't had time to create. The old man meets the young people and lives on" (IWWP, 22). This "living on" relates Williams to those who come after him as he had been related to his future self as a young man; his poems become the spiritual functions or endopsychic automatisms for the young's hopeless and desperate psychological states. But the very consciousness of this purpose forces Williams to invent some abstractable wisdom in his depiction of experience which, as he indicates in his view of a natural life for everything, including art, will eventually diminish or prove false. Until it does, it preserves what one can know of an effective tradition.

A psychological as well as a physical recovery from his cerebral attacks was needed before Williams could manage the range of reconciliations marking the conscious realizations of form in "Asphodel, That Greeny Flower" which ends his next volume, *Journey to Love.* W. D. Snodgrass' "Master's in the Verse Patch Again" (1964) describes it as a psychological recovery obtaining for American poets in general. "Our poets have a way of blossoming late," he observes, "often after a long sterile period. We have exciting enough early work, splendid last works, but little work of maturity—precisely that period when we might have expected the greatest work." He accounts for the phenomenon by suggesting that women wilfully prevent their husbands' becoming first-rate, and adds: "Often, only the approach of death can shock us from the trance of our life; we come to terms with *it* more courageously." [8] In the particular instance of Williams, he writes: "Williams truly loved his wife, yet spent years trying to injure her. Then, however, he could come back to her. Few have had his magnanimity which could forgive even someone he had so deeply wounded. After years of sterile literary dogmatism, it is to his wife that he comes back in his last great poem, 'Of Asphodel'—the flower that tells of his enduring love." [9]

Seeming to lend support to Snodgrass' position, Williams establishes his belief in the cruelty of love in "The Ivy Crown" (1954). Early in the poem, he announces, "The business of love is / cruelty *which*, / by our wills, / we transform / to live together" (PB, 125). Later, he repeats the sentiment: "Sure / love is cruel / and selfish / and totally obtuse— / at least, blinded by the light, / young love is" (PB, 126). In "Asphodel," he again claims that "I cannot say / that I have gone to hell / for your love / but often / found myself there / in your pursuit" (PB, 156). Moreover, by situating "Asphodel" during a brush with death, he seems to suggest himself as the model of Snodgrass' generalization. Yet, in the interval before "Asphodel," which Snodgrass designates as sterile, Williams was producing *Paterson,* and the poem is a significant production though, at the time, not the positive return to the dreams of his youth that Williams wanted his final statements to effect. Except operatively, it offered no new wisdom, no real alternative to the bomb, to the cruelty of love, to the destructive element of the Freudian id, out of which the imagination could build anew. This sense of failure or "despair" which the poet connects to a failure of language forms the barrier to a reconciliation with the world in *The Desert Music,* but disappears in the opening lines of "Asphodel" when the speaker comes "first to know / that there were flowers also / in hell" (PB, 153). These flowers—a longtime symbol of Williams and the poet—offset the divorce, the blockage, and the thematic failures of communication which run through *Paterson I–IV.* With their defeat, Williams could offer the beginning of Book III to *Perspective* in 1953 as "Work in Progress (Paterson V)."

That this psychological recovery may have evoked a memory of Dante for reasons other than Dante's "triple unity" is also possible. Williams had long associated the Italian poet with marriage. "Prose about Love" (1918) speaks of the Dante-Beatrice relationship in such terms: "Dante chose Beatrice who with all due allowance for mediaeval tenor of thought was his wife in exactly the sense I mean. To a man of spirit the loss of his chosen wife will be a spiritual catastrophe of such magnitude that he cannot envision it without experiencing at the same time a sense of insecurity extending down to the foundation of his personal consciousness." [10] The view is repeated in *The Great American Novel* (1923), which states that it is not possible for a poet to write about a poetic sweetheart and not about a wife: "All men do the same. Dante be damned. Knew nothing at all. Lied to himself all his life.

Profited by his luck and never said thanks. God pulled the lady up by the roots. Never even said thank you" (I, 166). Williams' close brush with death could have produced a reaction similar in magnitude but with the opposite effects of that produced in Dante by Beatrice's death. Such experiences are common enough, and the situation of the poem's speaker as either a Lazarus come back from the dead to tell all or someone visiting the dead supports such a belief.

Yet, by the time of "Asphodel" 's completion in 1954, Williams had clearly decided that the poem was not the specific form of "dying into art" that he wanted as the end of *Paterson,* however much "Asphodel" may have succeeded in the reconciliation of alienation which both Snodgrass and he associated with a first-rate work. The decision was made in spite of the poem's being generally regarded as his best. W. H. Auden called it "one of the most beautiful love poems in the language." [11] In "William Carlos Williams" (1963), Robert Lowell agreed, calling it a "great poem," "a triumph of simple confession," and "something that was both poetry and beyond poetry" (WCW, 159). In *Poets of Reality* (1965), J. Hillis Miller added his endorsement. For him it was "the extraordinary love poem of Williams' old age" and "a supreme attainment." [12] Likewise, in " 'A Certainty of Music': Williams' Changes" (1966), Richard A. Macksey cites it as "the last and perhaps the greatest of Williams' rites of passage" (WCW, 147). Even the author in *I Wanted to Write a Poem* refers to his delight in the poem's critical reception: "The one poem, 'Asphodel, that greeny flower' has been noticed and enjoyed by many people. The reviews of the book made me very happy" (IWWP, 92).

94

As life's dying into art was the theme of "Asphodel," the particular method of dying seems to have been a basis for the work's rejection as *Paterson V.* In "Asphodel," art had become the double of nature, a Demeter figure which rescued Kora from her sense of enclosure; but, in becoming this, the poem had reversed the poet's earlier aversion to preconceived outlines and, like the other parts of *Paterson,* had consciously accepted the ornamental, abstract bones of a form "put on ab exteriore." One notes throughout Williams' awareness both of other works of art, perhaps in an attempt to have his speaker embody a collective past, and of previous artistic formations of his own individual past. The fact that "Asphodel" begins as does Ezra Pound's *Cantos* in Book XI of the *Odyssey* and ends as the cantos were intended to in Dante's *Paradiso* suggests an immediate paradigm for it. And certainly some of the references to Homer owe more to Pound than to W. H. D. Rouse, whose translation of Homer Williams had encountered in 1951. But this is not to slight the poet's knowledge of either Homer or Dante. As he remarks in a letter to Frank L. Moore (1951), "The *Iliad* is a pure invention; the *Odyssey* is another. The *Divine Comedy* is another, though I reject it for the mist it invents to hide death from the eye which has bred that entire execrable horde of 'the church'" (SL, 297–298). Earlier he had called Homer "a subtle historian" and Dante "a great moralist" (VP, 30).

In this regard, Pearce's *The Continuity of American Poetry* rightly suggests that "Asphodel"'s invention must be regarded first as a kind of reply to Eliot, Pound, and Dante: "Elsewhere in the poem, against the Eliot of the *Quartets* and the Pound of the *Rock-Drill Cantos,* he challenges Dante and the whole history of Christian belief" (WCW, 103–104). The subscription to Joycean "mythic" form with its underlying view of cyclical, archetypal behavior that this challenge projects forms an alternative to the prophetic distancing which Williams uses to end the merging of art and life in the earlier books of *Paterson*. But missing the Einsteinian emphasis on light for the "radiance" of *Paterson*, Pearce wrongly goes on to note of the poem's "wisdom": "He declares that the true light is an inner one which only the poet, his verses vibrating with his own radiance, can turn on the world—and can then, and only then, receive a blessing from his world. . . . The world of the 'Asphodel' poem, and of other poems like it is full of one thing, the poet." "Knowing this," he continues in a further distortion, "who can the poet love but himself—or all those whom he can metamorphose into an aspect, or a function, of himself?" (WCW, 104). Certainly Flossie's attentiveness and closeness to the poet after his strokes can be interpreted as the love object's having become a facet of Williams, but only at the cost of an Einsteinian world which Williams acknowledges openly as his intent in two letters to Thirlwall and in his Sutton interview: "I've got myself in wrong before the critics by attempting to bring in the idea of mathematics. Of Einstein. Not Einstein, we'll say, but Einstein's ideas. The uncertainty of space." [13]

The parallel to Pound-Homer-Dante suggests, in addition, a remoter paradigm and another reason for the triadic line which in "Asphodel" approximates *terza rima* while the overall three-block structure suggests a Dantean *Inferno, Purgatorio,* and *Paradiso*. Williams' "Wallace Stevens" (1956) remarks that "subsequent to Dante's *Vita Nuova,* which marked a peak in musical verse, poetry forgot how to dance. English poetry . . . had not danced since the Reformation had bred Milton." [14] "Asphodel" is a poem about dancing, in both the celebratory and sexual senses of that word. The odd coda which disrupts its parallel to *The Divine Comedy* also, as Kenneth Burke's "William Carlos Williams, 1883–1963" (1963) remarks, disrupts the poem's organization. Forgetting Williams' remarks about "clean" language in his essay on Marianne Moore and in what he cites as "the most puzzling or puzzled contrivance . . . of the long late poem," Burke ponders: "To be sure, the flower is green, and that's all to the good. But a few lines before the close we are informed, 'Asphodel / has no odor / save to the imagination.' Yet in an earlier poem we had been assured: 'Time without / odor is Time without me.' And one of Williams' most amusing early poems was an itemized rebuke to his nose for the 'ardors' of its smelling" (WCW, 58). By adding to the threeness of the structure of the poem, the coda brings the world and worldly wisdom to the aromatic, sentimental, and nonmaterial drift of the previous sections. In so doing, it disrupts the unconscious structure of the poem's stream of consciousness by giving it in its final lines a conscious direction that makes possible the rejection of mysticism. The same rejection occurs in the poem that eventually comes to be *Paterson V* when the virgin of the imagination is whored by the reality of the world. Here the "whoring" is accomplished by drenching everything in the worldly absolute of the speed of light, but by this "drenching" the possibility of an unsatisfactory variance between unconscious and conscious structures is introduced.

Besides this use of reverberating artistic forms within a general stream of consciousness, "Asphodel" makes use of the same surfacing "collective" fact—contemporary and historical—that *Paterson* had to reinforce both an immediate sense of locale and the message of the work. Ralph Nash's "The Use of Prose in *Paterson*" (1953) had commented upon the particular device in the earlier books of *Paterson*. Yet, unlike them, "Asphodel" does not relegate these facts to prose. Everything is realized in the ethereal threeness of the triadic measure, even such unlikely items as the fire at the Jockey-Club in Buenos Aires which occurred on April 15, 1953. The *New York Times* reported that the fire "destroyed the club's famous collection of paintings by old masters, its priceless library and a wine cellar long rated as South America's finest." [15] On May 25, 1953, *Life* echoed the report of the destruction of a "priceless library and an art collection ranging from Goya to modern French masterpieces," [16] stressing the part of Juan Perón in sparking the riot. *Time* describes the rioters more graphically bursting "into the thick-carpeted clubrooms hung with Goyas, Corots, and Monets" [17] and makes the event, like Williams' report of it, clearly Perón-inspired. In "Asphodel," "with Perón's connivance / the hoodlums destroyed, / along with the books, / the priceless Goyas / that hung there" (PB, 168). Yet, unlike images in the early poems which could be verified in life, the *Catalogue Raisonné* (1950) of Goya's work lists only one painting, *Don Antonio Cobos de Porcel,* in the possession of the Jockey-Club, indicating that, unless it had acquired another Goya in the interval, only one Goya was lost in the fire. This suggests that the reader not rush to accept the seemingly impersonal elements of the poem as "facts." Their validity within the ethereal structure lies in their being paired off with other "facts"—often personal—within the work.

The same impulse toward and slighting of fact occur in the incidents which Williams adapts from his own previously realized *Autobiography*. Here he repeats techniques cited by Sherman Paul's *The Music of Survival* (1968) as common as well to "The Desert Music" (1951). The very asphodel which becomes the dominant image of the work derives from his stay in Switzerland in 1897: "There I first became acquainted with the native yellow primrose, so delightfully sweet-scented. The green-flowered asphodel made a tremendous impression on me. I collected all such flowers, as many as I found, and pressed them between the leaves of a copybook" (A, 29). In the poem, the experience becomes: "When I was a boy / I kept a book / to which, from time / to time, / I added pressed flowers / until, after a time, / I had a good collection. / The asphodel, / forebodingly, / among them" (PB, 155). The very closeness of the autobiographical account to the poem leads one to reject the incident's being weighed against Robert Graves's erroneous insistence in *The Common Asphodel* (1949) that the asphodel occurs in only one color—white. Nor is it any more helpful to verify the incident against the botanist's more liberal view of yellow and white asphodels. For the same reason of irrelevance, one might write off references to the asphodel in Book XI of the *Odyssey* and Williams' earlier uses of it in *Kora:* "For us heads bowed over the green-flowered asphodel. Lean on my shoulder little one, you too. I will lead you to fields you know nothing of. There's small dancing left for us any way you look at it" (I, 48). Going outside Williams' writings for its meaning, except perhaps to the Epistles to trace Williams' stylistic echoing of St. Paul, is not profitable.

A better alternative is *A Voyage to Pagany* (1928). Based loosely upon the poet's 1924 trip to Europe, the novel records an impression of "Sospel, like a bell, the bell of the asphodel, green, odorless—flower of Hades, flower of the dead" (VP, 87), and it is the bell rather than the petals of the flower to which the adjective "greeny" refers. Moreover, the allusion in Book II of "Asphodel" to the Jungfrau, obscured from view until "just before train time," has its affinity to Doc Evans' experiences at Interlocken in *A Voyage*. On the morning of his departure, "the Jungfrau showed its white breast" (VP, 231). No mention, however, is made of the waitress, who in the poem tells the couple that the mountaintop is visible. The account of the gypsy girl in Book II of "Asphodel" is similarly, but less faithfully, related to the *Autobiography:* "I broke away to the bare yellow hills back of the town, to be alone, to shake my shoulders from such impossibilities of past glory. There, or on the way down, rather, I was picked up by a gypsy girl, twelve or fourteen years old, with whom I talked innocently while she guided me out of the village paths where I had been lost" (A, 122–123). The incident which occurred in a 1909–1910 European trip becomes: "Starting to come down / by a new path / I at once found myself surrounded / by gypsy women / who came up to me, / I could speak little Spanish, / and directed me, / guided by a young girl, / on my way" (PB, 164).

Here, rather than the pairing off that the Goya incident undergoes, the singular fourteen-year-old is blurred into a collective "women," which echoes the blurring of Helen into all women, and, later, the discovery of a single man into the discovery of all men. Moreover, in the instance of Helen, who, as Martin P. Nilsson's *The Mycenaean Origin of Greek Mythology* points out, is a form of Kora, the bluring becomes a particularly fortuitous concinnity of conscious and unconscious elements. It makes her rape and the destructiveness of the Trojan War a parallel to the rape of spring and the subsequent sterility of Demeter's war with Pluto: "It was peculiar to Helen to be carried off, by Theseus and by Alexander. The rape of a goddess is a well-known feature in a special cult legend: Pluto carries off Kore. Though at first it may seem astonishing, the rape of Kore and the rape of Helen are in fact kindred, if we look away from the Helen of the epics and take her as the old goddess that she was; she is a vegetation goddess, just as Kore is." [18] The analogy which Williams never consciously applies to himself is one which Snodgrass seizes upon to typify American poets generally.

The manipulation of these collective and personal pasts within the unconscious and conscious structure of "Asphodel" is another matter. The flow of incidents begins with a celebration of the flower which the speaker is cheered to know grows also in hell. In this manner, the flower-filled life which he has lived with his wife may extend into death. The speaker's mind, thereupon, embarks upon an associative stream of fading flowers including the poor colorless asphodel he saw as a child in Switzerland. Although what he remembers is "too weak a wash of crimson . . . to make it wholly credible" (PB, 154), he dares not stop remembering or talking for fear of death, and, in an echo of "Young Sycamore" (1927), urgently asks his wife to listen. The principals resemble Aeneas and Dido in Book VI of the *Aeneid*, especially as forgiveness and the fear that the wife may turn away emerge as the work's opening themes. The speaker pauses to let his memories, like souls in Avernus, come "buzzing" like "a bee and a whole flood of sister memories" (PB, 154). Later, his loves like the parade of famous women in the *Odyssey* will become "a field made up of women / all silver-white" (PB, 160). The present flood, which is a recapitulation of earlier poems as well, serves the function assigned to memories in "Shadows" (1955): "That we experience / violently /every day / two worlds / one of which we share with the rose in bloom / and one, / by far the greater, / with the past, / the world of memory, / the silly world of history, / the world / of the imagination" (PB, 151). "The instant / trivial as it is," he continues, "is all we have / unless—unless / things the imagination feeds upon, / the scent of the rose, / startle us anew" (PB, 152). In serving this function, memories set up a structure of concinnity between experience and its explanation as well as of convergence similar to the concinnity and convergence of ideas in "Silence." Thus, they establish the theme of the present (sea surface) rescuing the past (sea depth) for a future by becoming the "white light" which lies at an intersection of blue and green and yellow and red. As *A Voyage to Pagany* had elaborated before, "The sea, giving up its history to the imagination" becomes "the accumulation of all time" and, as such, perfect (VP, 59). This "perfection" is conveyed structurally when the echo of a half-line from Spenser's "Prothalamion," introduced early in Book I, is completed late in the coda: "It will not be / for long. . . . 'Sweet Thames, run softly / till I end / my song' " (PB, 154, 181).

First gardens, then the sea, then books enter the lives of the speaker and his wife. With the last, enter Helen and

Homer and the Trojan War as a paradigm for all subsequent wars. The image of that war, transformed to heroism by art, requires a reinterpretation now if the imagination is to be cured and the will become again a garden. Toward this end, Williams begins to detail a new, experiential dialectic of war (death-desire) and love (libido) as once Homer catalogued Greek and Trojan forces and ships, hoping to learn something from the experience that might prove acceptable as art. The reinterpretation involves a consciousness of mythic literature which is unusual for the poet, but which, like the language of *Kora*, tries to be both subjective and objective. In the poem, the unconscious elements, because they follow the same pattern as conscious thinking, should not be too much at variance with the conscious. Yet what is apparent is Williams' desperation at evolving a structure the opposite of, yet as powerful as, Homer's and at the same time coming up with wisdom. The associations, which in stream of consciousness become a structure, reveal not so much a tendency toward a cold, impersonal shape as the speaker's reluctance to stop talking because talk acknowledges the presence of another, and the prospect of an individual confrontation with death is too terrifying to face. It is his hope that in all this talk something wise may emerge.

Book II continues the recollections, taking the figure up still nearer death. In it, the speaker announces that in order to understand the present one must find its key in the residual of earlier, wilder, and darker epochs. To know the significance of his death he must understand the makeup of its parts. This self-knowledge, which in mythic confrontation comes with one's facing the self objectified as the Other, herein, consistent with Williams' emphasis on social content and his own aversion to self-analysis, comes in the confrontation with a young man. Asking a young visitor—perhaps meant to be a double of himself or a symbol of the future—what interests he has, he hears that the young man has liked "Between Walls" and has heard of "On Gay Wallpaper," early Imagist poems and consecutive selections in *Selected Poems* (1949). The conversation leads him to ask his wife to help him recall their trip to Europe and the Jungfrau, which his mind associates immediately with an earlier European trip and the mountains near Granada. The memories seem to be set off as oppositions to the young man's interests in India. The impatience of the young man reminds him, too, that death begins in the head, in the imagination, when in pursuit of wealth it invents the bomb—"also a flower"—and forgets the sea. A new dialectic begins with Charles Darwin, who worked for the betterment of all men by projecting man's origin, opposing him to Ethel and Julius Rosenberg, who by divulging the secrets of the atomic bomb made man hostage to its powers of destruction. Moving to more national concerns reminiscent of *In the American Grain* (1925), he then pits Columbus' discovery of the New World and its subsequent personal disappointment against Cotton Mather and the more disappointing witchcraft trials at Salem. Finally Williams opposes the politics which inspired the destruction of the Goya at the Jockey-Club with his own human preservation of a painting by Charles Demuth. This last is an instance of the humanity which, rather than ideology, lay at the base of his politics.

Book III begins with the power of forgiveness to bring sanity back to a world gone insane, or spring to a winter world. So, in the winter of both the year and the speaker's life, a similar restoration may exist "if one can find the secret word to transform it." A sequence of episodes evolves to tame the "crude" brute animal force (id) suggested negatively by Colleoni's horse (war) and positively by the mare in *Venus and Adonis* (love) and imaginatively by the train (technology). For the task, a "wise old man" is enlisted. He is "a man of perhaps forty," with "a black beard, and a hat." He reminds the speaker appropriately of his father or his own double. The speaker, caught in the repetitiousness of his own unconscious, knows, "He / will know the secret" (PB, 173), but, before he can obtain the secret, the old man is gone, and with him the successful entry to the Jungian "door of the future." His appearance and leaving recall the full and faded flowers, enlisting recollections of the romantic primitivism of Herman Melville and the real darkness of the Cro-Magnon cave artists. Unable to separate ideas from things and thereby learn great wisdom from experience, he awaits the spring flowers, the turn upward, asking to be cured of past hurts and the trance that holds men like rats to the cupidity of an invisible Pied Piper of Hamelin. Thinking of the pride that motivates these men, he turns to homey flowers—the daisy, the small yellow sweet-scented violet—and lets them become the "facts," "poems," and proper fields of imagination. But here, where stream of consciousness ends, the thematic need of Williams to evolve wisdom from experience defeats the fused operative and thematic modes of the poem by trapping him into believing that wisdom is somehow transcendent, and he moves out of predicaments (things) into their lessons (ideas).

The coda takes up these "lessons" by taking up the problem of "light" (knowledge) which outlasts the "fire" (heat of life) but which is also a medium of experience and the absolute to which, in Einsteinian terms, all things are relative. This "light" "gelds the bomb, / permitting / that the mind contain it" (PB, 179). Too, it forms the equal of love and the imagination as the "ungodly" Williams' trinity: "Light, the imagination / and love, / in our age, / by natural law, / which we worship, / maintain / all of a piece / their dominance" (PB, 180). It is the "act" to the thunderstroke's "emotion" between which falls not an Eliotic shadow but spring. In an Einsteinian universe, it should prove as rich as was the darkness (sin/superstition) which John Donne probed, replacing the thunderclap (Zeus, God) as a sign of divinity, but also, in keeping with the threeness of the poem, lacking a fourth element. In an Einsteinian universe, it should replace as well the thunder with which *The Waste Land* concludes and reverse that poem's return of poetry to the academy. By light's measure, the medieval world becomes humane. It can be enjoyed for its pageantries, its light, pomp, and ceremony, and not for its preoccupation with mysticism.

Like the poem's other threads of a collective unconscious, these pageantries can be seen as racial autographs. As early as Marsden Hartley's *Adventures in the Arts* (1921), Williams was aware of this aspect of pageantry, and he had used Hartley to give support to such works as *Spring and All* (1923). Writing of the Indian, Hartley had said: "It is our redman who permits us to witness the signing of his autograph with the beautiful gesture of his body in the form of the symbolic dance which he and his forefathers have practiced through the centuries." [19] In a scientific and therefore essentially female age, as Williams describes it in "The Great Sex Spiral," the autograph will assume scientific properties: "Light," the medium through which the present communicates to a future, becomes the present's "dance," penetrating, as the asphodel—now without odor—begins to, into all crevices of the speaker's mind. Thus, the major poem of Williams' late years ends with a celebration of an absolute in Einsteinian light. Being of worldly and scientific origin the light is not the Divine Light of Dante's *Paradiso;* it is, nevertheless, in its pervasiveness an equivalent to it. "Vs." (1948) had asked: "If we wish to find again the seriousness of the Delphic Oracle and sense again the awe it inspired, if the devotion of the Crusaders, and the valor of Richard Coeur de Lion is to be known; if the Spanish mystics are to become again credible, and the very sainthood of the early martyrs to be realized, the magic of Papal Infallibility believed, where shall we look in our day?" Williams had maintained that "we shall find it in all its pristine innocence, in all the glory of its devotional appeal, but especially in the seriousness and vigor of its original character, in only one place in our modern world, the daïs where science sits enthroned." [20] Yet, like Dante's *Divine Comedy,* the celebration fails to bring the world, the devil, or Pan into its resolution, and Burke, in finding the coda puzzling, is right in feeling that it opposes the poet's earlier views.

On the basis of the satyric dance and the whoring of the virgin (imagination) which came eventually to stand as the final wisdom of *Paterson V,* Williams' other conscious use of the Kora pattern, one can hypothesize that, in his rejection of "Asphodel" and its interweaving of mythic form as *Paterson V,* Williams wanted to remain truer to these earlier dreams. Rather than the cold, intellectual abstraction of science, he wanted a situation whose dance as in *Kora* "is in following now the words, *allegro,* now the contrary beat of the glossy leg" (I, 55). For such a purpose, not only is the "mystical" triadic structure of "Asphodel" abandoned, but the book is dedicated to the "memory of Henri Toulouse Lautrec," who with his paintings immortalized the whores of Montmartre. No Einsteinian light here, but the sacramentalizations of life in the wedding of male and female and in Williams' early metaphor of the dance: "We know nothing and can know nothing / but / the dance, to dance to a measure / contrapuntally, / Satyrically, the tragic foot" (P, 278). This final "ignorance" is the paradoxical knowledge on which his writing began and which, in "hopeless and desperate situations," had first prompted the dream formations of the "wise old man" and the unconscious Kora and Orpheus patterns. By returning to it, he, in effect, returns poetry to its beginning in the dance, to his anointment by his "grandmother," and to the unconscious as the final knowledge, much as Joyce's knowledge in *Finnegans Wake* (1939) returns the reader to the beginning of the book.

In this connection, one might interpret the malaise of the American experience for which Snodgrass is searching as the consequence of not finding the wisdom which the image of the old man or Demeter promises to the pre-reflective consciousness. Like James Fenimore Cooper's Natty Bumpo or Williams' own Columbus or Eric the Red or Daniel Boone, the discoverer must go on discovering, for to stop is to become the victim of the herd which follows. Despite age and infirmity, Williams must enter again the cycle and repeat the process, showing in its repetition that, as he pretends to wisdom, the "wise old man" is a charlatan, or at best a Sisyphus whose pursuit of knowledge becomes the only knowledge. Becoming less sure in age, he must resort more and more to skepticism or put on the masks of institutional knowledge (science, religion, formalism) to bring his experience into a pattern (abstract understanding). One thinks, too, of the various intellectual absolutes, including Roman Catholicism, which American artists have toyed with in their maturity as easy ways toward such patterns; and one ponders whether perhaps only a self-reflexive direction and process of individuation can offset this waiting for the disappearing father and lead to the calm assurance of experience reconciled with its explanation. It is clear that Williams could not for long exist in the Edenic state which the Prologue to *Kora* associated with his mother. Her ability to be "incapable of learning from benefit or disaster" because she could see "the thing itself without forethought or afterthought but with great intensity of perception" (SE, 4, 5) was after a few years of writing closed to him. *Pictures from Brueghel* (1962) proposes that the calm may come with the poet's acceptance of the circle as a metaphor of knowledge and his being satisfied not with ultimate wisdom but with this metaphor. One no longer enters the dance, but describes others in the process of dancing and talks of one's need to join in.

Within the distinctions of voyant and voyeur that Richard Ellmann draws in *Eminent Domain* as the poles of modern literature, Williams thus chooses the role of voyeur. As in his choice of language earlier, the selection seems motivated partly by his dual role as physician and poet. As the *Autobiography* relates: "In illness, in the permission I as a physician have had to be present at deaths

109

and births, at the tormented battles between daughter and diabolic mother, shattered by a gone brain—just there—for a split second—from one side or the other, it has fluttered before me for a moment, a phrase which I quickly write down on anything at hand, any piece of paper I can grab" (A, 289). So, too, within the distinctions of soldier and philosopher which Joseph Conrad draws in "Youth: A Narrative" (1902), Williams chooses to be the soldier. "I remember," Conrad has his narrator say, "I preferred the soldier to the philosopher at the time; a preference which life has only confirmed. One was a man, and the other was either more—or less." [21] Williams clearly wanted only to be a man, but like his heroes Columbus and Eric the Red, he wanted to be a man to the fullest. In so wishing, he could not completely abandon the antithetical, love-hate, psychic figures of Dante, Eliot, and Cotton Mather.

CHAPTER FOUR

Sex and the Williams Poem

※ In 1946, William Carlos Williams wrote his "Letter to an Australian Editor," expressing his opposition to Ezra Pound's view that mind "fertilizes mind, that the mere environment is just putty," and that man, "since Joyce discovered Hamlet, is out to seek his own father— his spiritual father, that is." [1] Instead, he proposed that "there may be another literary source continuing the greatness of the past which does not develop androgynetically from the past itself mind to mind but from the present, from the hurley-burley of political encounters which determine or may determine it, direct." [2] He went on to note, "We must acknowledge to ourselves that the origin of the new *is* society, that each society not only originates but fertilizes its whole life, of a piece. . . . If a man in his fatuous dreams cuts himself off from that supplying female [society], he dries up his sources—as Pound did in the end heading straight for literary sterility." [3] A year earlier in "The Fatal Blunder" (1945), Williams had accused T. S. Eliot of a comparable wrong-headedness for proposing in "Ash Wednesday" that "what is actual is actual only for one place." The accusation asserts, "Look at your feet and you will know what is actual and at the same time universal, that you exist, the universal in the particular. . . . It is in the universal diversity of place that the actual gets its definition and vigor and that love itself is generated. . . . [W]hen we experience an actuality, when we experience a vivid moment of passion, associated as it must be with some place, . . . then, our sensibilities kindled, the knowledge that another in a different place, associated with another complete paraphernalia shares with us this experience, then a literature is born." [4]

Long before Williams had made these connections of poetry and sex or the decision in *Paterson I* (1946) to make that city the poet's place and female source of inspiration, he had begun to delineate what he perceived to be their intimate relationships. A digression in *I Wanted to Write a Poem* (1958) makes it appear that a connection between the two, expressed in terms of art's organic relation with the life about, was already formed by the time *The Tempers* (1913) was published. Williams tells Edith Heal, "Somehow poetry and the female sex were allied in my mind. The beauty of girls seemed the same to me as the beauty of a poem" (IWWP, 14). But a little later, commenting on *Al Que Quiere!* (1917), he relegates the book and its clear sexual preoccupations to "a quiet period, a pre-sex period, although I was married" (IWWP, 23). Certainly the connection has been made before the publication of *Kora in Hell* (1920) and that book's alternation between word and glossy leg. For its cover Williams had selected an "ovum in the act of being impregnated, surrounded by spermatozoa" (IWWP, 28), and scattered throughout the volume are numerous references to sex and poetry.

A temptation exists to suppose that originally Williams' position may have had something to do with Remy de Gourmont whose work and brilliance Pound had been championing to the young writer-doctor since at least 1913 and against which Williams was to react in the Prologue to *Kora*. Gourmont's famous *Physique de l'amour* (1903) was to be translated in 1921 by Pound. Pound acknowledges in his Postscript an acceptance of Gourmont's view on sex and intellect: "Il y aurait peut-être une certain corrélation entre le copulation complète et profonde et le développement cérébral." [5] Pound goes on to add: "Not only is this suggestion . . . both possible and probable, but it is more than likely that the brain itself is, in origin and development, only a sort of great clot of genital fluid held in suspense or reserve. . . . This hypothesis would perhaps explain . . . the enormous content of the brain as a maker or presenter of images." [6] Pound ends his discussion by announcing, "It remains that man has for centuries nibbled at this idea of connection, intimate connection between his sperm and cerebration. . . . The liquid solution must be kept at right consistency; . . . the balance of ejector and retentive media." [7] Many of the metaphors for intellectual activity used by Williams in the letter agree with this view, but one can as easily associate the position with Walt Whitman, whose "raw vigor" Williams claims to have admired along with "the studied elegance of Keats" before he met Pound (IWWP, 8). In poems like "I Sing the Body Electric" (1855), Whitman had equated the human body with

113

poetry and the dynamics of poetry with the body in sexual activity.

Williams' own explanation of the position's source in Otto Weininger's *Sex and Character* (1903) occurs in his modifications of Dora Marsden's "Lingual Psychology." Writing to *The Egoist* (1917), he used the occasion of her call for a new philosophy rooted in particulars to register his own thoughts on the matter. Reducing her "philosophy" to male and female psychologies, he goes on to say of the first: "Male psychology is characterized by an inability to concede reality to fact. This has arisen no doubt from the universal lack of attachment between the male and an objective world—to the earth under his feet—since the male, aside from his extremely simple sex function, is wholly unnecessary to objective life. . . . Thus the male pursuit leads only to further pursuit, that is, not toward the earth, but away from it—not to concreteness, but to further hunting, to star-gazing, to idleness." "Female psychology, on the other hand," he notes, "is characterized by a trend not away from, but toward the earth, toward concreteness, since by her experience the reality of fact is firmly established for her." He concludes the two-part modification by taking issue with Weininger: "Man is the vague generalizer, woman the concrete thinker, and not the reverse as he imagined." Williams then praises the "far-reaching and indestructible service" of both Weininger and Marsden in having recognized that "the psychologic field" is divided "into reciprocal halves, the cleavage running roughly with the division into sex," and adds of Weininger that "he seeks to discover a third gender as the type to be approached." [8] Yet, despite an added rejection of Weininger's asceticism, Williams seems to subscribe to the German's view that "the man of genius possesses, like everything else, the complete female in himself." [9] "Transitional" (1914) announces: "It is the woman in us / That makes us write" (CEP, 34); and *A Voyage to Pagany* (1928) has Grace Black tell Doc Evans: "You are a curious mixture, Dev. There are two parts: that hard clearness which is your inner core and makes you go, and the tenderness of a woman" (VP, 211).

In *Kora,* Williams had followed a view of beauty standing on the edge of the deflowering with "I confess I wish my wife younger. This is the lewdest thought possible" (I, 59). He had gone on thereafter to present the poet as a satyr in pursuit of a dryad, a figure no doubt derived from Keats's images of Phoebe in *Endymion* (1818) and of Poesy in "Sleep and Poetry" (1817). The satyr will return to close *Paterson V* (1958) nearly forty years later. Keats's dryad, whom depth psychologists might associate with the anima, shares, like Williams' figure, in the anima's standing "for the loyalty which in the interests of life" the man "cannot always maintain; she is the vital compensation for the risks, struggles, sacrifices which all end in disappointment; she is the solace, for all the bitterness of life. Simultaneously, she is the great illusionist, the seductress who draws him into life—not only into its reasonable and useful aspects but into its frightful paradoxes and ambivalences where good and evil, success and ruin, hope and despair counterbalance one another." [10] The effect of the anima is to give "relationship and a relatedness to a man's consciousness." [11] But the view of sex and poetry which the anima suggests and which images the preobjectivist call for an integrated cycle of life and art does not provide for the organic inner life of an art work and cannot be called sexual in quite the same way that Hubert in *Many Loves* (1942) calls verse, "the drama of words—words in love, / hot words, copulating, drinking, running, / bleeding" (ML, 33).

This organic, sexual cycle of poetry and life is the principal theme of *In the American Grain* (1925) and *A Voyage to Pagany*. In them the love of a white man (satyr) and Indian (dryad) becomes an emblem for the wedding of the male psyche to the soil (female psyche). "The Three Letters" (1921) had earlier personified America as the grandmother-feminine-godhead-virgin-whore-Kora-Demeter figure of "The Wanderer" (1914), and repeatedly *In the American Grain* asserts, "The blood means nothing; the spirit, the ghost of the land moves in the blood, moves in the blood" (IAG, 39). Women are identified as "givers," as "closer to earth—the only earth" (IAG, 181); the Indian maid, Jacataqua, is epitomized as their ideal. As Williams acknowledges, "If the land were to be possessed it must be as the Indians possessed it." Such possession means that "the characteristic of American life," its holding off "from embraces, from impacts," in order to gain, "by fear, safety and time . . . its object just out of reach" (IAG, 175) must be rejected. What America has gained is the "annunciation of the spiritual barrenness of the American woman" (IAG, 181) in a male to male tradition whereby "men are trained never to possess fully but just to SEE" (IAG, 175). America has an Albert Pinkham Ryder with "no detail in his foregrounds just remote lusts, fiery but 'gone' " and a "moonlight" Edgar Allan Poe (IAG, 181). Williams wishes to counteract the annunciation by telling poets that their function is similar to that which Jacataqua assumed in

her time, by giving, as she had, actuality to man's con-
ceptual capacities. His final image of Abraham Lincoln
as the American ideal, "a woman in an old shawl," recalls Weininger's androgynetic genius as well as Williams'
modification of that genius into the poet.

Similarly, Doc Evans, the hero of *A Voyage to Pagany*,
on landing in Europe cries within himself for *la France*,
"as if expecting to see some symbolic image of joy rise
from the ground and stride forward carrying flowers in her
hand" (VP, 8). Instead, Grace Black, the American Indian
living in Vienna, convinces him that he should return
to America. The novel, which owes considerably to the
Williamses' trip to Europe in 1924, owes as well structurally to Keats's *Endymion*, especially in the relationship
of Evans and his sister. Here, despite obvious analogues
to the "brother and sister against the world" theme of *Die
Walküre*, the novel's resolution more nearly resembles the
independent salvations of Endymion and Peona than the
opera's secret forest lodge and its resultant Siegfried. Moreover, the book's various women, Lou Martin, the German
Venus, and Grace Black, formed as fragments of Flossie
Williams, recall the various appearances of Phoebe in the
Keats poem. Less obvious to a reader is the way the book's
balancing of Dante and Whitman looks backward also
to a male "mind to mind development" and Williams'
remarks in "America, Whitman, and the Art of Poetry"
(1917): "There is no art of poetry save by grace of other
poetry. So Dante to me can only be another way of saying Whitman. Yet without a Whitman there can of course
be for me no Dante." [12] Williams' promise at the end of
the essay to study Dante leads to Evans' trip to Italy and
to the book's final acceptance of America and Whitman.

117

Thus realized in the book's indebtednesses are the two modes of love which the novel at various moments blurs. At one point, Williams has Evans ponder: "There are no two kinds of love. Love is love. The moralist will tell you that. You love some one, that is all. If you love a girl, you want to have a baby. If you love a man, you want to have—what?" (VP, 24). At another, the lovers, Dev and Lou, are approaching "Marseilles, the city of sailor love," "awed by the sea, giving up its history to the imagination" (VP, 59). What is most revealing about the first instance is that sexual activity for Williams inevitably must contain at least the possibilities of procreation, even male love. He begins his discussion of what male love might produce by speaking of love among brothers: "How do men ever get on without some business together? Brothers never do" (VP, 20). The discussion moves to the love of a father: "Evans thought of his English father. How the devil do you love a man anyway? Either you slop over or fight or else you avoid each other" (VP, 20–21). The discussion then moves to the love of friends: "Evans needed Jack. Jack had rescued him in America, rescued him from much stupidity, from dullness, at a time when he needed just that" (VP, 22). Finally, it deals with occasional, perverse love: "You might as well pick up a sailor" (VP, 23). The offspring, business and art, which make possible men's getting along with one another, are for Williams the reasons for supporting such allegiances. In a letter to his son (1942), he repeats the case rather poignantly: "That relationship between father and son is one of the toughest things in the world to break down. It seems so natural and it is natural—in fact it's inevitable—but it separates as much as it joins" (SL, 201). The success of the relationship lies, as Williams reestablishes, in its generative nature, in a son's evolving an independent style.

For the purposes of such male to male offspring, *A Voyage to Pagany* is willing to admit "that art is a country by itself" (VP, 251), and *In the American Grain* laments the impulse toward perversity when such relations—here among women—are not regenerative. "One of the hottest women" Williams had ever known, "lascivious in what might have been the sense in which I speak of it, but too timid, unable to stem the great American tide inimical to women, spent almost the whole war period in Washington. . . . The girl's passion was horrible to behold. It turned slightly later, though she didn't perhaps perceive it, to other women" (IAG, 184). The failure of "animate touch," which he attributes as the cause, also turns the Puritan into a sodomite: "One had not expected that this seed of England would come to impersonate, and to marry, the very primitive itself; to creep into the very intestines of the settlers and turn them against themselves, to befoul the New World" (IAG, 68). Its promulgation into a perverse economics is scored in "Pound's Eleven New 'Cantos'" (1934): "Then, suddenly, in Canto XXXIX, there is disclosed an unfamiliar magnificence of fornication—the official sin of constituted stupidity. That sex will be accomplished in sin, is the blind behind which venality has worked to undo the world. Kids may go masturbating into asylums but profits must be preserved. . . . The mind of man is dwarfed by the buggery of professional thought. The understanding thrives on a fornication which bespeaks an escape of the spirit to its own lordly domains" (SE, 168).

Thus, sexuality is not necessarily opposed by its perversion but by a sexlessness which Williams on occasion refers to. *In the American Grain* speaks of the Aztec priests' "ceremonial acknowledgment of the deep sexless urge of life itself" (IAG, 34), and "Inquest" (1947) explains: "You take a woman's body and make it do what it was never meant to do and it's the dance. It really is. Sexless. Only when you make it sexless can it properly express sex. Because it isn't sex any longer. It's the dance" (FD, 320). This "dance," which may be achieved by a successful, self-conscious negation of sexuality, is also the Crocean preconscious intuition toward expression. This intuition lacks the sexual differentia which "How to Write" (1936) relegates to the "fore-brain." The essay most openly presents Williams' views of the mind and the mind's relation to writing in terms of what James Joyce called "the he and she of it." It describes a ritualistic, amoral, "deepest mind," as well as a "deeper" middle brain. This deepest mind has affinities to Carl Jung's racial unconscious; it is sexless. Already the middle mind has begun to assume sexuality with its portions of personality, and the sexuality is further defined by the fore-brain. As associated with writing, the qualities of mental process defined here constitute a refinement of those characteristics of male and female psychologies which Williams wrote of in *The Egoist* and are to be found underlying his criticism of that period. In short, he makes a high degree of abstraction and form male and the obverse female.

Within the early poems, Williams translates these views of sex and poetry into sexual imagery and rhythms. "Drink" (1916) describes a "feel of good legs / and a broad pelvis / under the gold hair ornaments / of skyscrapers"

(CEP, 140), and "Winter Quiet" (1917), fences "tense with suppressed excitement / . . . where the ground / has humped an aching shoulder for the ecstasy" (CEP, 141). "Virtue" (1917) refers to the "steaming phallus-head / of the mad sun himself" (CEP, 152), and "Arrival" (1920) pictures an autumn undressing for sex. "The Cold Night" (1921) connects the April sky to "the round and perfect thighs / of the Police Sergeant's wife" (CEP, 203), while "Horned People" (1923) and "The Avenue of Poplars" (1923) depict boys of fifteen and seventeen as "dirty satyrs . . . vulgarity raised to the last power" (CEP, 203) and leaves embracing in the trees. "Rigamarole" (1924) sees the moon "in the dark oak tree's crotch" (CEP, 278), and "The Source" (1928) repeats the image with the sharp elm leaves shaking "in the crotch / brushing the stained bark / fitfully" (CEP, 346). "Della Primavera Transportata al Morale" (1930) further posits a squirrel in the crotch of a maple tree and a woodpecker in a sycamore's hole. Its sun is "ovoid," and like the embracing leaves of "The Avenue of Poplars," fierce winds lash its "long-limbed trees whose / branches / wildly toss" (CEP, 64). "The Flower" (1930) becomes "at its heart (the stamens, pistil, / etc.) . . . a naked woman, about 38, just / out of bed" (CEP, 237), and finally "stript sentences" in "The Botticellian Trees" (1931) move "as a woman's limbs under cloth" (CEP, 81).

Less overt sexual connections appear in the handling of machines, power, and thought. "The Revelation" (1914) begins a long association between automobiles and seduction that carries through "The Young Housewife" (1916) and "The Italian Garden" (1960). Having established a relation between women and nature or an attraction to the machine, each poem then violates this relationship, often

121

by having a car crush the frail object that wed it to woman. Similarly, the expanding power of the city in "The Flower" is shown to violate the countryside, already identified as "a naked woman." "A Good Night" (1916) uses the sounds of police whistles, traffic, and machines as an inducement to sleep and seduction, and "At the Faucet of June" (1923) shows J. P. Morgan and the power of money as the seducers of Persephone. The power of social prestige becomes the means for the rape of the downtrodden in "Impromptu: The Suckers" (1927), and more consistent with the views of his *Egoist* pieces, Williams, in poems such as "The Unknown" (1940), "The Last Turn" (1941), and "Raindrops on a Briar" (1947), opposes the male conceptualizing power to feminine detail. "Writer's Prologue to a Play in Verse" (1940) sums up the results: poetry must not be "masculine more than it is / feminine"; it is not "a book more than / it is speech" (CLP, 151).

This final hermaphroditic state, like the equilibrium of art and life which *Kora* defines, is what Williams wished to have his art achieve. Continuing the metaphor of the machine, the telephone—because of its design or a connection with language—becomes hermaphroditic in "The Hermaphroditic Telephones" (1923), and, echoing "Writer's Prologue," eye and ear bed down together in "Song: Beauty is a shell" (1960). This last conveys a kind of aestheticism whereby one shapes the future (vision) to what one has heard. Nevertheless, the images of the writer and art as androgynetic lead significantly to an association of both with flowers and the sea. The clearest case for the androgynetic nature of flowers is made in the four poems which, in *I Wanted to Write a Poem*, Williams states he created along still life motifs. Flowers, as all gardeners know, have both "male" stamens and "female" stigmas. Rarely are the two organs in contact when they are both ripe, and cross-pollination is usually achieved by wind, insects, water, and birds. If cross-pollination has failed, self-pollination can take place when, at the end of the flower's life, the style curls back so that the stigmas are brought into contact with their own pollen. This knowledge lies in back of the male-female sexual imagery gracing "Daisy," "Primrose," "Queen-Ann's-Lace," and "Great Mullen" (1920–21). The first admits to being both masculine and feminine: "He lies on his back— / it is a woman also" (CEP, 208); while "Primrose" with its "sepals curled / backward into reverse spikes" (CEP, 209) suggests a flower in self-pollination. "Queen-Ann's-Lace" describes its feminine sounding blossoms under sexual attack by the more masculine "wild carrot taking / the field by force" and leaving "wherever / his hands have lain . . . / a tiny purple blemish" (CEP, 210). The last, "Great Mullen," not only pictures its flower as bisexual but surrounds itself with a male cricket and a cow so that the sexes of the three principals get confused in he-she referents.

"The Sea" (1923) extends this view of hermaphroditism to the wooing that penetrates "to the edge of the sea" and "returns in the plash of the waves." Its generative source is the dark where "there is no edge / so two" (CEP, 275–276). From this wooing of planes, "The Sound of Waves" (1948) has emerge like Venus "above the waves and / the sound of waves, a / voice · speaking!" (CLP, 172). This voice becomes the poem, and, as "Asphodel, That Greeny Flower" (1954) asserts: "The poem / if it reflects the sea /

reflects only / its dance / upon that profound depth / where / it seems to triumph" (PB, 165). This profound depth is doubtlessly the same sexual dark of the earlier poem, indicating the same sort of androgynetic generation that Williams, by the end of Book III of "Asphodel," associates with facts, flowers, and poems. In fact, all the works of the imagination become sexually charged and interchangeable by means of an almost Crocean coalescing of expression with the middle and forebrain stages of intuition. In "To Daphne and Virginia" (1953), Williams enlarges on the earlier equation of poetry and science that "Notes from a Talk on Poetry" (1919) made to assert: "A new world / is only a new mind. / And the mind and the poem / are all apiece" (PB, 76).

Nevertheless, the collecting of his poems for *The Complete Collected Poems* (1938) seemed to have marked some kind of turning point toward sex in Williams' life. As he told Edith Heal, "This was a period in my life when I was tremendously interested in women. I had never been a roué and women remained an enigma; no two had the same interest for me; they were all different. I was consciously interested in too many of them; and trying to find out about them all" (IWWP, 64). In particular, Williams was trying to find out about his mother, whose sayings he had been collecting for years (SL, 163) and with whom he had embarked upon a translation of Quevedo. In one of his sketches for the introduction to the translation, he notes: "A woman creates a son, and dies in her own mind. That is the end. . . . If in a son one could live again! But it is impossible. And if you [the son] make it a work of the imagination, she might have said, it won't be me." Williams protests that her survival will not be "a work of

the imagination," [13] indicating thereby that their male-
female collaboration on the Quevedo might constitute the
effort. In addition, as a letter to Robert McAlmon asserts
(1939), Williams was reemerging from one of the "winters"
of his marriage. He was appreciative anew of his wife:
"Floss is worth having lived to discover—and she seems
to have lived through it for me" (SL, 181).

But what is most revealing about what he tells Edith
Heal is the connection he makes between sex and survival. He announces, "All I can say is man is only *hors de
combat* if he is such a poor specimen he couldn't be of
interest to anyone" (IWWP, 64). The statement reminds
one of the subtitle for Charles Darwin's *The Descent of
Man: A Selection in Relation to Sex* (1871), the "survival of the fittest" notion of Herbert Spencer, which
Darwin incorporated into later editions of *The Origin of
Species,* and Williams' repeated assertions of having read
the books avidly, with great aftereffects (YMW, 8; IWWP,
13; A, 15; I, 215). Williams' views on sexuality seem intimately connected to a comparison of the artist's struggle for survival to that struggle of the species. The notion
of poetry which emerges as "hot words, copulating" in
1942 goes even further in this direction. The work of art
has realized, because of its reproductive capacity, an existence like that of a work of nature, but independent of nature. As "A Beginning on the Short Story (Notes)" (1950)
will make evident, art works "are creations. Natural objects. Not copying. But by housing a spirit, as nature
houses juice in an apple, they live" (SE, 303). Williams
then goes on to cite the practice of Braque that his *Autobiography* (1951) would associate with the demise of art as
mirroring and the advent of Objectivism: "Braque would

take his pictures out of doors and place them *beside* nature to see if his imitations had *worked*" (SE, 304; A, 240–241). The notion has corollaries also in what I. A. Richards means by the "interaction" of words.

Independently of Williams but perhaps drawing upon a common source in the *Phaedrus* (277), Richards uses Plato in a lecture at Princeton in the Spring of 1941 to explain that by "interaction" he means "words, which are competent to defend themselves, and him who planted them, and are not unfruitful, but bear seed in their turn, from which other words springing up in other minds are capable of preserving." [14] Richards goes on to add that Plato was fond of dealing with language in such metaphors and that, as they took on analogues to animal reproduction in his *Republic,* they achieved "a frankness which embarrassed his Victorian translators." Moreover, the very definition he gives to words in the lecture has strong analogues to Williams' views: "Words are alive as our other acts are alive. . . . A word then by this sort of definition is a permanent set of possibilities of understanding, much as John Stuart Mill's table was a permanent possibility of sensation. And as the sensations the table yields depend on the angle you look from, . . . so how a word is understood depends on the other words you hear it with." [15] This pragmatic position, which in the matter of word definition—though not of language function—may seem different from Williams', has its origin in Charles Peirce's assertion that words have different meanings not because of some direct res-verba relation but by virtue of use: a chair used as a weapon is different from a chair used to sit on.

Consequently, in *Many Loves,* when Peter complains that the fault of Hubert's writing is its inability to complete the sex act, Williams in fact is talking about a failure of language: "Here, in / the third act, when the business should be / primed and waiting. . . . / It won't stand up. Stand up, you understand. / Kick and yell and drive in as / it should—any proper scene / nearing the catastrophe must do" (ML, 88). Similarly, when the hanging of John Johnson at the close of *Paterson IV* (1951) produces a blast of semen, Williams is asserting the way words ought to work to bear seed in their turn. The sperm of a poem should be equivalent to life sperm. Words here should lead to *Paterson V*, to other words in other minds. But this fertilization is not like that of Richards—an inner life based upon "sentimentalism," upon what connotation of words adds to connotation; rather, for Williams, language's sexuality is the product of its sources.

By analogy, sexuality seems to suggest to the poet a wedding of the male language of thought and art and the female language of life to produce the complex eye-ear idiom that Lowell praises in "William Carlos Williams" (1963). Earlier, Williams' "Robert Lowell's Verse Translation into the American Idiom" (1961) had used similar terms to compliment Lowell's versions of Charles Baudelaire: "That they are not classroom English I take for granted. That they are something more akin to the local American way of speaking, in other words to what we hear every day makes him our fellow." [16] The suggestion of an interacting written and spoken language appears, too, in the mingling of diction that, shortly before his death, Williams described for Stanley Koehler (1964): "I couldn't speak like the academy. It had to be modified by the conversation about me. . . . Not the speech of English country people, which would have something artificial about it;

not that, but language modified by *our* environment; the American environment." [17]

Furthermore, in the light of Williams' other discussions of father-son relationships, one can assume that part of his need for a generative Anglo-American language was based firmly on a desire to achieve a style independent of his father, an Englishman by nationality. *I Wanted to Write a Poem* speaks of writing as something that the poet associated with his mother (IWWP, 16); *Yes, Mrs. Williams* (1959) notes the elder Williams' intense liking for Shakespeare (YMW, 8); and the *Autobiography* tells of a dream that occurred a few days after his father died "after a wasting illness, on Christmas Day, 1918": "I saw him coming down a peculiar flight of exposed steps. . . . He was bareheaded and had some business letters in his hand on which he was concentrating as he descended. I noticed him and with joy cried out, 'Pop! So, you're *not* dead!' But he only looked up at me over his right shoulder and commented severely, 'You know all that poetry you're writing. Well, it's no good.' " (A, 14). To write in the anglicized style of Pound and Eliot would be to write in his father's idiom, and, as "America, Whitman, and the Art of Poetry" had said concerning Whitman, "The only way to be like Whitman is to write *unlike* Whitman." [18] The proper way to honor one's father was to do something that would stand intrinsically along side his accomplishments, and this, as Williams' letter to his son and his Prologue to *Kora* maintain, requires novelty.

Thus Williams' rejection of the "sterile" mind to mind development of Pound and Eliot occurs specifically so that he might assert in part his own being in a counter literary technique. As early as his review of Norman

Macleod's *You Get What You Pay For* (1940), he had begun to emphasize designs that would balance male and female approaches, and the emphasis helps to explain the presence of the six letters from a woman writer in *Paterson II* (1948). They give to the book an important feminine balance that has been too little recognized. Critics have tended to either ignore the passages, paraphrase them, or damn them. Thomas R. Whitaker believes that the last eight-page letter stops the book's progress; Lowell refers to them as "chunks of prose"; and Randall Jarrell questions that any amount of context can justify them. Ralph Nash's "The Use of Prose in *Paterson*" (1953) defends them, but on rhythmic rather than psychic grounds. The letters appear two to each section, and a seventh letter introducing "C." occurs early in the first section of *Paterson I*. All, as the final, long letter asserts, rely upon distinctions which Williams made in his piece on Anaïs Nin, "Men . . . Have No Tenderness" (1942). They also resort to a technique that the poet used for depicting his mother in "Raquel Helene Rose" (1941); he lets the writer present herself rather than risk "some antagonism, some self-defense" that "seems to rise out of a woman when a man tries to understand her" and a self-conscious awareness that she may be "there ready to tell me I've got her all wrong" (IWWP, 65). In addition, they have recourse to the various portraits Williams drew earlier of his English grandmother, Emily Dickinson Wellcome.

The Nin essay speaks of the "many special difficulties" that women in the arts have had to overcome. Foremost is a time lag between the respective ascendancies of man and woman to intellectual distinction. It "placed woman too much on the defensive in a world lacking much that she had to offer." [19] What this is that woman offers is focus, expressed in language echoing Williams' *Egoist* letters: "The male scatters his element recklessly as if there were to be no end to it. Balzac is a case in point. That profusion you do not find in the female but the equal infinity of the single cell. This at her best she harbors, warms and implants that it may proliferate." [20] Second, she offers a method of composition that reverses the values which men hold. What Miss Nin achieves is the female counterpart of Williams' notion of no ideas but in things—things in pursuit of ideas. He quotes approvingly her description of "the dream . . . always running ahead of one. To catch up. To live for a moment in unison with it, that was the miracle." [21] So, at the onset, when "C." sends Dr. Paterson her first note, she confesses "to be more the woman than the poet" and to be concerned "less with publishers of poetry than with . . . living" (P, 15). Already mention of "public welfare workers, professional do-gooders and the like" has made her a victim of the social system (P, 16). The circumstances suit ideally Williams' preconceptions of the psychology of the female writer. Moreover, as "C." will rightly insist, in a man-created poem feminine segments by their very placement will be distorted into something else.

The second appearance of "C." occurs in the opening section of *Paterson II.* Amid Paterson's assertion of his mind's need to come to terms with the female world outside and the various images of marriage, violence, and sterility, she speaks of a "kind of blockage," an "exiling one's self from one's self" (P, 59). This exiling is explained by another letter which demonstrates a limited ability to accept the world outside. Whereas she can understand Z.'s failure to accept her as a poet, Paterson's failure bespeaks a failure of intersubjectivity, a failure to be recognized as a poet by one who pretends to know of women writers. It constitutes, therefore, the kind of masturbation D. H. Lawrence describes in *Pornography and Obscenity* (1929): "Enclosed within the vicious circle of the self, with no vital contacts outside, the self becomes emptier and emptier, till it is almost a nullus, a nothingness." [22] It is a "complete damming up" of all her creative capacities (P, 59). Preceding Klaus Ehrens' long sermon and the Hamilton passages, her next appearance in Section II shows her as Eliot's counterpart. As he in "Ash Wednesday" restricted actuality to one place, she restricts identity to one person: "There are people—especially among women—who can speak only to one person. And I am one of those women" (P, 80). Williams, on the other hand, not only insists that actuality be rooted in several places but that his knowledge of himself come from knowing many women. Thus, one can understand how he might view her position as an unacceptable equivalent of Eliot's. Classic symptoms of what R. D. Laing would call "ontological insecurity" emerge with her next appearance. That sense in the ordinary circumstances of living that one is more unreal than real, more dead than alive, prompts an image of "crust"; it is an instance of "petrification," a case of her fearing depersonalization by others, of her having been turned into an object. She complains of indifference, of impersonality, of needing to break through a film or crust into a true self.

Her last two appearances in Section III comprise a bitter indictment against Paterson's failure to understand his "fellow man, except theoretically—which doesn't mean a God damned thing" (P, 101). So, as the male mind finds the night and nature seductive to poetry, she works to jar him back to "reality." First, she writes, her letters were interesting to him "in so far as they made for *literature* . . . , as something disconnected from life" (P, 105–106), but, once her life entered, he grew aloof. She asserts that, unlike him, she cannot separate her life from her writing; social conditions must be set in order before her writing can be set in order. She reviews their relationship and his attempts to aid her and compares the effect to that of a patient suffering from pneumonia who has been given "a box of aspirin or Grove's cold pills and a glass of hot lemonade" (P, 110). With this comparison, the submerged intent of her correspondence begins to surface. Paterson has tried to secure her a job, but as she could not remedy her writing faults until social conditions changed, she cannot accept work until she has clothes and money.

At this point her protestations that she cannot ask him for assistance are rendered hollow by her past and present actions. The letter instances, as a consequence, the distortion of language which a perverse society allows and offers striking support for her insecurity by emphasizing her preoccupation with preserving rather than gratifying herself. Paterson has failed to secure her book review assignments and a fellowship at Yaddo, and she has failed, too, to land them on her own. She holds him somehow accountable for the resultant situation, and, in a new effort at intimidation, attempts to impress him with her literary past. The letter concludes with their real point of difference: she attacks him for confusing "protection from life with an inability to live"; he is "thus able to regard literature as nothing more than a desperate last extremity resulting from that illusionary inability to live" (P, 111). In short, she accuses him of being "male," of having a concept of life to which he expects his experiences to conform. In contrast, she offers a mode of experiencing that is not prejudicial, and to which one brings one's understanding. She feels that she may become grist for his vanity—"a flower in his buttonhole"—and concludes with the clearest evidence of her falsity: she will forgive him "if some of the things to which I have called your attention here should cause any change of heart in you regarding me" (P, 112).

A first of three postscripts goes on to tell of the unlikely incidents surrounding the loss of Paterson's first money order to her. She identifies herself as "Cress" and, on the basis of a letter to Marianne Moore (SL, 233), Whitaker's *William Carlos Williams* (1968) argues rightly for Chaucer's Criseyde. But Shakespeare's "false Cressid" may be intended as well. Troilus' dismissal of her letter as "Words, words, mere words, no matter from the heart, / The effect doth operate another way" (V,iii,108–109) seems to foreshadow Paterson's reaction. This initial postscript ends with mention of the need for a typewriter, and it is followed by another note calling the earlier rhetoric "the simplest, most outright letter I've ever written to you." The eight-page document then concludes with a plea for serious attention to what she has written "out of fairness to me" (P, 113). Throughout the long account she has explained in order to accuse, understanding neither the drift of the Nin essay to which she refers nor what Williams' means by "the failure of language." She has violated his first principle of writing—"straight expression"—for a kind of devious pleading that he associates with the worst women writing. She never lets Paterson know what she wants or the conditions on which she will accept his aid.

Mrs. Wellcome, too, had "blackguarded her oldest son / into buying" a piece of property (CEP, 172) and had seemed to claim any empty house as hers because she needed it. Her assertion in "Portrait of a Woman in Bed" (1916) that she would not starve "while there's the bible / to make them feed me" as well as her warning—"Try to help me / if you want trouble / or leave me alone" (CEP, 151)—anticipate "C.'s" responses to others' relationships with her. Similarly prophetic is the grandmother's transformation into Elsa von Freytag Loringhoven, the Baroness of the *Autobiography* and the letter-writing "La Baronne" of "The Three Letters." As "C." had written Paterson, she writes Evans, the hero of the tale, "out of a clear sky asking for help." Like "C.," La Baronne lived "in the most unspeakably filthy tenement in the city" and "was a Bohemian," [23] and finally, like "C.," she ends by writing a series of infuriated and abusive letters. The *Autobiography* describes the Baroness' pursuit of the poet and his giving her "two hundred dollars to get out of the country" but, like Paterson's first money order, "it was stolen by the go-between" (A, 169). Moreover, as Mrs. Wellcome had become Williams' Demeter in "The Wanderer," one can see in "C.'s" letters indications of her assuming the anima function that the feminine portion of the male psyche is thought to effect. "C." does try to preserve Paterson's connection with life, and she does try to give relationship and a relatedness to his consciousness. That she fails is indicative of her own illness rather than of a difference in roles. Similarly, she takes on the role of Kora assigned by Williams in *Kora in Hell,* and itself another image of completion through art. Her long last letter has provided Paterson with another world into which he might descend if he so chooses so that, by a "sickening turn toward death," its pieces might be joined into art. That Paterson chooses not to descend at this time —except by the suggestion in the phrase "La votre C." that *Paterson II* bears some oblique connection with *Troilus and Criseyde*—is significant. One purpose of including a letter in *Paterson I* had been to provide such choice, and here it spells some kind of regression into previous art.

Yet what Williams may have wanted to produce by including the letters was "a stasis, an absolute rest," which "Men . . . Have No Tenderness" associates with a balance of male and female psyches. The "stasis" would prove Williams' ability to present a female psyche. If any "marriage" of Paterson with "C." is to evolve from this stasis, he may want it to occur not on the page but in the minds of his readers. A similar feature of balance occurs in his biography of his mother, *Yes, Mrs. Williams.* After a series of biographical sketches, Williams again tries to let the woman present her character through scraps of conversation, notes, letters, proverbs, and asides. Begun ten years before the publication of *Paterson II,* the book did not see print until a year after *Paterson V* was out. Its improvised nature reaffirms the sense that the lack of design is intentional, a harking back to his old definition of woman as the concrete thinker whose failure when she fails is that of design not of detail. By emphasizing detail to the detriment of design, the book pretends to approximate a female way of thinking; yet the very imitative fallacy behind both presentations—a mirroring of mental processes

rather than objects in order to assert an inner *Geist*—
throws Williams' theory of art as imitation into question.
He complained of the biography in a letter to Winfield
Townley Scott (1959) that "I can't keep from telling you
that it will be far from a finished book when it is finally
released—too many people have had a hand in its composition and I am powerless to do anything about it. At that
Dave [McDowell, the publisher] has done what he has had
to do or there would have been no book at all." [24]

This indecision about the worth of his mother's biography led to its coming out ten years after his mother's
death, and Williams may have suspected on reflection a
comparable weakness of design in the *Paterson II* episode.
Despite his preoccupation with the need for art to balance
male and female psychologies, he gives no other woman
"C.'s" freedom to define herself in *Paterson*. These women
—Phyllis, Corydon, Mme. Curie, Mary, the virgin of the
unicorn tapestry—appear as parts of his structure. Furthermore, what he consistently recalls as the most significant achievement of the particular book is not the presentation of "C." but the discovery of the variable foot and
triadic line in the poem's third section. Three years after
Paterson II appeared, in a review of *The Mills of the
Kavanaughs* (1951) he expressed sympathy with similar
organizational difficulties in Lowell's title poem. Praising
the work, he singled out as its main achievement a triumph
over a failure of design: "It is to assert love, not to win it
that the poem exists. If the poet is defeated it is then that
he most triumphs, love is most proclaimed" (SE, 325). Yet,
as "In Praise of Marriage" (1945) suggests, an emphasis on
male and female psychologies may be too limited. Even at
the time of writing *Paterson II*, Williams may have al-

ready shifted part of his concern to language. Reminding readers that the title of Kenneth Rexroth's *The Phoenix and the Tortoise* was a variation on Shakespeare's poem on marriage, Williams goes on to comment: "But, of course, 'turtle' in that [Shakespeare's] case means dove. But Rexroth specifically means what he says, 'tortoise' and no bird. I say it's odd, this interplay between two languages in the title, the English and the American—and hard to tell just how far Rexroth wanted to carry the analogy." [25]

In some ways, by virtue of its necessary distancing the largest and most important wedding—that of the poet with society, "that supplying female"—dissolves into the background of these more primal unions. This wedding, too, undergoes changes from what it was in *Kora,* moving from an idea of society's independence from art to one of society's and man's mutual redemption through the poet's finding a "redeeming language." In these areas Williams is most willing to make his concessions to Pound—though not to Eliot. Pound had brought to the present "news of those great societies of the past" by which the present might be enlightened, and, as "Convivio" (1949) affirms, despite a common tendency to forget at times that they are of the same brotherhood, their "wealth / is words. And when we go down to defeat, / before the words, it is still within and / the concern of, first, the brotherhood." The poem urges that their most effective blows be reserved "for the enemy, those / who despise the word . . . who decree laws / with no purpose other than to make a screen / of them for larceny, murder—for our / murder" (CLP, 209). Still, *Kora* attacks deracinated nationalism, calling Pound "the best enemy United States verse has" (I, 26), and underlying the accusation are two views which, in realizing the union and its intended end, complement Williams' approaches to psychology and language. First is a view of the poet and culture similar to that which naturalists posit for man and his environment. Part of man's character is determined by his ability to adapt to his environment; so, too, is part of a writer's skills. If he is an American writer, this means his adaptation to an American culture. Second is the belief that what America offers the writer by virtue of its peculiar culture is a chance at novelty, a chance to give birth to something different from and perhaps equal to the great objects of the past. This last allows in artistic terms for Pound's subsequent view regarding societies that the present "capitalist imperialist state must be judged not only in comparison with unrealized utopias, but with past forms of the state; if it will not bear comparison . . . either as to its 'social justice' *or* as to its permanent products, art, science, literature, the onus of proof goes against it." [26]

Yet, for Williams, if man could not go back comfortably to earlier stages of evolution, the artist could not go back comfortably to older ages. *The Great American Novel* (1923) repeats the emphases on novelty, place, and time, naming Europe and the past as America's great enemies: "The background of America is not Europe but America. . . . Europe's enemy is the past. Our enemy is Europe" (I, 195, 209–210). "In Praise of Marriage" warns the reader that "the only thing we can take bodily from the past is the seriousness of the past, the refusal to lie, the refusal to accept anything that has not been tested by the BEST brains of the time. Seriousness today must be tested or retested on PRESENT knowledge." [27] Survival, he might have added, can only occur in terms of the sole reality there is, the present. "A Good Doctor's Story" (1937) supports Williams' statement that he "tried to follow the teachings of Major Douglas" (SL, 339). It complains of *The Citadel*'s vision that "what Dr. Cronin doesn't see is that, as Ezra Pound would say, it's money and its misappropriation and artificial scarcity that are at the back of our troubles, and that unless you see the thing through to its source you can see nothing," [28] and later, Jarrell's "A View of Three Poets" (1951) will lament Williams' introduction of "Credit and Usury, those enemies of man, God, and contemporary long poems" [29] in *Paterson II*. But, as, for the naturalist, adaptation to one's environment often requires generations, so, too, regardless of disadvantages, one's acclimatization to culture cannot occur overnight. Gurlie tells the other characters of *White Mule* (1937): "We didn't come here for love of the country, only to better ourselves. How can we love this country? We are from Europe. That's our country. That old love of home strikes to the second and third generation. That's why America is all for greed. This wasn't our land. It belonged to the Indians. It will take a long time to get a love for it like we had on the other side" (WM, 238).

This subordination of society to redeeming language in his final years led to Williams' continuing attacks on the public secondary schools for their failures to teach methods proper for survival. "The American Idiom" (1960) describes the situation: "Every high school in America is duty bound to preserve the English language usage as a point of honor, a requirement of its curriculum. To fail in ENGLISH is unthinkable!" His alternative is to have the schools teach "the language we speak in the United States." [30] In literature, Williams wanted to replace the cultural standards that had been imported from Europe with an agreed-upon sanctuary where works in the American idiom could proliferate and engage in their own evolutionary struggle for existence, toughening and progressing and adapting, until, after a time, the best of them would be able to compete with the best of Europe and the past. This could not be done by burlesquing the language as Pound had. Revising his earlier view that Pound "writes in American as far as he writes in any language" (SL, 132), Williams told Walter Sutton in "A Visit with William Carlos Williams" (1961) that Pound tended to clown "in a Yankee farm accent" as had James Russell Lowell: "He clowns it so obviously that . . . no one would ever talk that way." [31] The clowning destroys the generative potential located in real American speech; survival could be accomplished most effectively by strenuous, attentive, "serious" listening.

Despite these shifting views on the relationships between art and survival, Williams remains consistent on the artist's procreative role in the process. "Sermon with a Camera" (1938) claims that "the artist must save us. He's the only one who can. First we have to see, be taught to see. We have to be taught to see *here,* because here is everywhere, related to everywhere else." [32] "Image and Purpose" (1938) adds that the poet must not forget "that it is words that are his materials and *not,* as a poet, states of society. . . . Not that states of society and the conditions governing words cannot be semblable but you *cannot* write a poem paying primary heed to social conditions, you cannot write a poem with anything but words, words that will do their part, as much as words can do." [33] Both positions are close to that which Pound ventured in "How to Read"

(1929): "The individual cannot think and communicate his thought, the governor and legislator cannot act effectively or frame his laws without words, and the solidity and validity of these words is in the care of the damned and despised *litterati*. . . . When their work goes rotten . . . the application of word to thing goes rotten, . . . the whole machinery of social and of individual thought and order goes to pot." [34]

But whereas Williams' move was from an interest in society to a consideration of language, Pound grew more and more to believe that economics and government took priority. Williams records of his visits to St. Elizabeth's: "Naturally we could not avoid the perennial subject, economics and the convictions . . . that it is international finance that brings us all at always shorter and shorter periods to our ruin. That wars are made by the international gang . . . and that in the present instance F. D. R. was the prime criminal. . . . In many cases I can see the justice of his views, both in that particular, regarding the criminal abuse of the functions of money, as well as the place of the poem in our attack; it is a basic agent in putting pressure on the blackguards who compel servitude, abetted by the various English Departments of 'the university' with their 'sacred' regard for a debased precedent" (A, 336, 341). Often Williams disagreed with the particulars of Pound's extreme positions regarding language and government, and, as late as 1956, he was still writing Pound, "We weren't governed by crooks, as you persist in saying, but by men who had to employ the instruments that were ready to hand; that they were not revolutionary geniuses may be true but they had a going country on their hands and many enemies such as you had to deal with" (SL, 339).

Foreshadowing his stand in "Convivio," Williams wrote to Pound in 1946 that he understood perfectly the poet's adult concern for government, discipline, and his courageous defiance of the spurious. "But," Williams went on to add, "you make an ass of yourself for all that. . . . [I]t was stupid of you to attack the President of the United States as you did—plain stupid. . . . Nevertheless, right or wrong, government is a major subject for the aging poet, and your work strikes along the path with some effect, if weak since . . . you talk about things, . . . instead of showing the things themselves in action" (SL, 249–250). What one can sense emerging from these positions and exchanges is Williams' clear reluctance after "The Three Letters" to give full recognition to the sexuality implicit in his view of a sustaining maternal society. If culture—land and tradition—nurture the poet and, in turn, must succumb to him in order for art to be created, one gets the most basic psychological myth imaginable— the oedipal myth—on which many psychologists posit the figure of the androgyne. As Jung's *Symbols of Transformation* asserts, "He who stems from two mothers is the hero: the first birth makes him a mortal man, the second an immortal half-god." [35] The two "mothers" are often Demeter and Kora, mother and anima, and their lurking at the edges of Williams' consciousness of sex and poetry fits perfectly with the baptism in the "filthy Passaic" that "The Wanderer" described as Williams' entrance into poetry as well as with the fantasy seduction by America in "The Three Letters." Thus, when Pound asked his old friend "why a world dominated by such a theme" as the debasement of man by usury should "look for love's subtleties or even its absence or presence," almost in reaction to the implied relationships of the myth, Williams responded: "The poem is a capsule where we wrap up our punishable secrets. And as they confine in themselves the only 'life,' the ability to sprout at a more favorable time, to come true in their secret structure to the very minutest details of our thoughts, so they get their specific virtue. We write for this, that the need come true, and it appears to be this which makes the poem the toughest certainty of continued life that experience acknowledges" (A, 337, 343).

Later, Williams was to add, "There is one thing God Himself cannot do. . . . He cannot raise the arm and lower it at the same time. . . . Therefore duality, therefore the sexes. Sex is at the bottom of all art. He is unity, but to accomplish simultaneity we must have had two, multiplicity, the male and the female, man and woman—acting together, the fecundating principle" (A, 373). But that one would not think sex determined everything in his work, Williams often complained when others did not recognize his intellect (CLP, 65, 95; A, 390). Moreover, as if to defend his profundity and maleness against these accusations, he told Sutton of his reaction to jazz: "If you've got to be sexually excited about it, it shows you to be a boob. It merely excites; there's no subtlety at all. . . . I wanted always to be conscious, I didn't want to indulge in sex so much that I lost my head." [36] Consciousness, as "America, Whitman, and the Art of Poetry" had asserted decades before, was for Williams the prime and continuing requisite of freedom. He never retreated from his view that the artist must ever be able to "recognize whither he is trending, and to govern his sensibilities, his mind, his will so that it accord delicately with his emotions." [37] This was so even if the artist—as had Williams—altered the directions in which he trended, and even, too, if he did not know the exact direction of every individual effort.

CHAPTER FIVE

Brueghel: Descent Once More

⚜ In providing pieces of art that would go beyond him into the lives of the young, William Carlos Williams takes up in his final books a problem which he had thought to solve in 1928 by his Objectivist theory. The theory asserts that past objects like the sonnet, having about them past necessities which have conditioned them and from which, as a form itself, they cannot be freed, must give way to objects consonant with the present; no art will long endure the attacks on its vitality which time makes. Yet, by taking as the central image of *Paterson V* (1958) the presumably still viable, centuries old Verteuil tapestries at The Cloisters, he casts doubt on the validity of this older view. His inability to part irrevocably with past pieces of art forms a confusion comparable to that which results from his inability to dissociate himself completely from the antithetical love-hate figures of Dante, T. S. Eliot, and Cotton Mather. In the title sequence of *Pictures from Brueghel* (1962), he adds to the confusion by basing his poems on ten sixteenth-century panels. Moreover, as if to emphasize a personal element in this change of views, he de-

votes one poem, "The Painting" (1960), to a portrait
which his mother executed while she was an art student in
Paris and which became his after her death. All of these
actions seem extensions of the autotelic descents which
moved him in the poems written after his 1952 cerebral
attack from present into past and back into present, reviving in the process the "abandoned movements" of
youthful dreams that he believed necessary to the phenomenal world of a writer's last years if he is to be considered "a master." All seem part, too, of his efforts
through design to impose a masculine sensibility on feminine detail. The reader meets, as a consequence, a new,
late, and seemingly further ideological snarl in a poetic
canon whose dialectic is already characterized by contra-
diction, vacillation, and reversal.

How much this snarl has to do with the poet's physical
condition is problematical. Denise Levertov's "William
Carlos Williams" (1963) tells how at the very last "he
could hardly speak, could no longer read to himself, [and]
typed with one hand with great difficulty." Nevertheless,
except for her final visit with him several weeks before his
death in 1963, he would repeatedly astonish her "with his
vitality, his shrewd humor, his undeviating, illuminating
attention to what concerned him—the poem, the poem,"
and she would "leave the house in a state of exhilara-
tion." [1] Justifications like Ralph Waldo Emerson's warning in "Self-Reliance" (1841) that "a foolish consistency is
the hobgoblin of little minds" [2] or Walt Whitman's em-
bracement of contradictions in "Song of Myself" (1855) are
entirely possible; but, for Williams, the distinctions which
Søren Kierkegaard makes in *Either/Or* (1843) regarding
ethical and aesthetic choice prove more appropriate. Ethi-

146

cal choice, Kierkegaard points out, is an absolute choice between good and evil, whereas "aesthetic choice is either entirely immediate and to that extent no choice, or it loses itself in the multifarious. . . . When one does not choose absolutely one chooses only for the moment, and therefore can choose something different the next moment." [3] Williams' tendency is to see statements, as William James in *Pragmatism* (1907) sees theories, as *"instruments, not answers to enigmas in which we can rest."* [4] He seems constitutionally incapable of accepting for long a procedure in art as consistent as the one he used in medicine, a procedure which might subject his material to a "lifeless ritual." He had written John Riordan as early as 1926 that "my whole effort . . . is to find a pattern, large enough, flexible enough to include my desires. And if I should find it I'd wither and die." [5] Williams may and often does change his beliefs.

Moreover, with the writing of *Paterson,* he had begun to merge art and life into "environments" or "contexts of experience," in which the sharp delineations usually drawn between the experiences of nature and art began to blur. The "sameness" of the new experience which would radically alter, if not destroy, art form as form would mute Objectivism's major attack on outmoded form and lend weight to statements like that contained in *In the American Grain* (1925): "That of the dead which exists in our imaginations has as much fact as have we ourselves" (IAG, 189). It would also explain his reference in *Paterson III* (1949) to books being "men in hell," forcing a resemblance of finished art to both the natural hell out of which his discoverers Columbus and Daniel Boone rescued knowledge and the imaginative hell he resorted to in order to

147

write. Likewise, the intended "sameness" would account for his excitement in a letter to Ralph Nash after Nash had pointed out in "The Use of Prose in *Paterson*" (1953) that the work's shift from poetry to prose was "a forceful marriage of his poem's world with that world of reality." [6] As Williams wrote Horace Gregory in 1944, the "marriage" would entail making self a part of art form.

Still, this proposed integration does not mean that there is no confusion in the belief the poet offers in these final volumes or no history attached to his position. The fusions of art and life which he would make on one level are undermined or negated on another by distinctions which he continues to make between their effects. For example, he seems perfectly aware that the weavers of the tapestries, whom he mislocates in the twelfth century, were not mirroring life, that their threaded imitations of flowers, by becoming nature, caught up the scenes outside as "real" flowers do and encouraged the many poems which possessed him. He also seems to be aware that art offers a relief from the inundations of life and therefore cannot be the same as life. Yet, his new emphasis on art form's being integral to personality will not permit him to make the distinctions which Jean-Paul Sartre makes in *Literature and Existentialism* between literature's "live" and "dead" states. One may no longer write as writers did in previous centuries because their language does not lend itself to modern experience, but as Williams' attacks on John Donne suggest, one could not simply and dispassionately pronounce a writer "profoundly and deliciously wrong." [7]

For Williams as for Ezra Pound, art, science, and literature became permanent products of the state and, along with the state's "social justice," the bases on which states would be judged. Their permanence, again not always distinguishable from form, lay in the very way they colored the present—often in terms of the state's being "a second body for the human mind" (P, 116)—and Williams' preoccupation with literature, science, and art as indications of Paterson's development as city and as man reflects the centrality which he assigns their suasive powers. Moreover, as the history of culture became for Pound the history of ideas in action, so, too, did it for Williams, except that for Williams, because of a view of sex, ideas passed through an intermediary stage of "things." No ideas, he insisted, but in things, but things in action, and Charles Doyle's "A Reading of *Paterson III*" (1970) affirms that much of the revision of that book was to make static scenes active. Nonetheless, "things" do have form and, if Williams' Objectivist theory was correct, these forms in time must be subject to decay.

The roots of these inherent confusions can be traced to the almost diametrically opposed positions on art which the poet takes over his long career. "Yours, O Youth" (1922) is almost neoclassical, stressing the objective character of great art, equating it with nature, and advising young writers to study the masters. This location of art outside the imagination extends to the poems, in the reverence he shows Brueghel in "The Dance" (1942) or Homer and Dante in "Asphodel, That Greeny Flower" (1954). One may also note it in *The Selected Letters* (1957), in the various compliments he extends over his lifetime to other works of art. Conversely, by using other texts one might hold that the old man who will meet the young people in art and live on lives not by any objective survival of art but by the way in which he is subjectively absorbed, enlivened, and distorted by the young. In this instance, Williams' belief in death as a thematic end to *Paterson* as well as his ending it originally in prophecy becomes a temporary lapse. He had always provided in his works for propagation or the incorporation of past objects into new contexts; *In the American Grain* offers proof of this as does the prose of *Paterson*. Yet the stress on those incorporations was on the art work, and it is clear that the emphasis is now to be put even more subjectively on the artist. His statement to Edith Heal in *I Wanted to Write a Poem* (1958) is that the old man, not the piece of art, lives on, and, although *Paterson III* expresses some uncertainty about "which is the man and / which the thing and of them both which / is the more to be valued" (P, 140), one must assume that he was being truthful with her.

Thus, what is indicated by *Paterson V* and *Pictures from Brueghel* is not quite a reopening of the problem of the immortality of art so much as a new probing of the immortality of the artist by virtue of his art. The emphasis is to be put not on the poems or their sexuality but on the intelligence shaping the poems and, as if to point up this stress, Williams chooses subjects for them that make incontrovertable his indebtedness. Both books use established art works to explore those instants when experience crystallizes into artistic inspiration, and in both books, as in the set pieces of one's art school training, mastery lies not in the choice of subject but in the artist's skill at execution. His mother's painting, he notes, is not original, but that of a child with "a delicate lock of blond hair dictated by the Sorbonne" (PB, 27). Similarly, in "The Adoration of the Kings" from "Pictures from Brueghel"

(1960), the set-piece character of Brueghel's work is established: it is "a scene copied we'll say / from the Italian masters" (PB, 6). Yet Williams denies this indebtedness by insisting that there is "a difference" both in "the mastery / of the painting / and the mind the resourceful mind / that governed the whole" (PB, 6).

Since by the example of the panel and his comments on its successes Williams tends to suggest his own work and the way he would like it approached, readers ought to allow in their views of Williams a comparable awareness of a work's difference from its source. The approach he invites is similar to that which, in Ann Winslow's *Trial Balances* (1935), his friend Marianne Moore proposed for the poetry of Elizabeth Bishop: "We can not ever be wholly original. . . . Nevertheless an indebted thing does not interest us unless there is originality underneath it. Here, the equivalence for rhyme, achieved by coming back again to the same word, has originality; and one feels the sincerity, the proportionateness, and the wisdom of superiority to snobbery—the selectiveness." [8] Instead, the poet received comments like those of Charles Olson, whose *"Paterson (Book Five)"* (1959) complained, "My difficulty with the new poem was that the tapestry, even if the poet called it 'the living fiction,' was a tapestry—a sewn cloth of flowers, a white one-horned beast, and the dogs which hunt it," [9] and of A. Frederick Franklyn, whose "The Truth and The Poem" (1963) compared the Brueghel sequence to the "stronger" poems of the volume and found in them a "quality of a pretentious kind of finger-exercise on the piano." [10]

Those who did compliment the books—for example, Robert Creeley, Hugh Kenner, and Denise Levertov—

tended to make language and measure the bases of originality, often completely ignoring the changes that, as proof of his own "resourceful mind," Williams wrung on the "original." All accepted unquestioningly a view of the poet as a "transliterator" of painting similar to that which Bram Dijkstra's *The Hieroglyphics of a New Speech* (1969) enunciates. There, commenting on Williams' use of Fra Angelico's *Annunciation* for "March" (1916), Dijkstra notes: "This description set a pattern which Williams continued to follow faithfully in poems of this kind: he records the details of the images presented by the painting in the order of their visual importance—in the same order, in other words, in which, on seeing the painting, his awareness would register them." [11]

Given the intended stress of both *Paterson V* and *Pictures from Brueghel* on the intelligence shaping a work of art, Williams' choice of central images proves enormously rich. The Verteuil tapestries have a long and clear history, and *Paterson III* makes passing mention of them before the poet takes them up later in the work. James J. Rorimer's *The Unicorn Tapestries at The Cloisters* states that five of the tapestries "were in all probability made for Anne of Britanny (1476–1514) in celebration of her marriage to Louis XII (1462–1515)." The other two, "somewhat later in date . . . may have been added to the original set when Francis I married Anne's daughter and heir in 1514." [12] The legend of the unicorn which they depict is also old. Rorimer notes, "In the Middle Ages it was believed that the unicorn could be caught only by a virgin. It was related that this wild and unconquerable animal became tame when confronted by a maiden; he would lay his head in her lap and was easily taken by the hunter.

The story of this hunt was used as an allegory for the Incarnation, the unicorn being a symbol of Christ, the maiden the Virgin Mary, and the huntsman the angel Gabriel. In time, the legend of the unicorn caught by a maiden came to be associated with allegories of courtly love." [13] In the case of Anne, who was a widow, Rorimer asserts, "At this time, as in the Renaissance, the unicorn was associated with marriage as well as with virginity." [14] Carl Jung's *Psychology and Alchemy* treats the legend as an expression of the paradoxical nature of the anima (the female element in the male unconscious), repeating the medieval association of the hunt with Christ and the Holy Ghost. Jung assigns it an "extremely intricate and tangled connection between pagan natural philosophy, Gnosticism, alchemy, and Church tradition." [15]

For Williams, the legend of the virgin courted by the unicorn is not quite an expression of any of these ideas. At times, as Doc Thurber illustrates in *A Dream of Love* (1949), the figure comes close to Jung's anima. Doc tells his wife that, in order for man to protect his integrity as a man, he had to "create a woman of some sort out of his imagination," for "just as a woman must produce out of her female belly to complete herself—a son—so a man must produce a woman, in full beauty out of the shell of his imagination and possess her, to complete himself" (ML, 200). Earlier, *In the Money* (1940) had had Doc Mabbot confess to Gurlie: "I always wanted a girl. I always wanted to play with her, dress her, undress her, put her to bed, watch her run around the place and grow up—there's a lot of woman in most men . . . in doctors anyhow—a lot of woman" (IM, 138). Nevertheless, as Doc Thurber makes clear, the hunt is also at times an allegory for secular incarnation, a making of the word flesh. It is the "thinging" of ideas, associated not with Christ but with the escape and Kora myth which Williams consciously and unconsciously spent most of his life elaborating. The "satyric dance" that whores the virgin of the imagination and ends the episode is the same dance that occurs in *Kora in Hell* (1920) and weds life and poetry by "following now the words, *allegro,* now the contrary beat of the glossy leg" (I, 55). Likewise, it is the dance mentioned by Williams in "An Essay on *Leaves of Grass*" (1955) as "the origins of our verse."

Thus, by secularizing and aestheticizing the myth of the Incarnation, Williams individualizes the traditional allegory of the hunt given by Rorimer and Jung. The courting of the virgin becomes a myth for writing and perhaps also—in view of the failure of institutional religions—a way of making writing into a religion and the writer's living on a substitute for Everlasting Life. The equation of the artist and unicorn in Part I of the segment supports such a view: "The Unicorn / has not match / or mate · the artist / has no peer" (P, 246). So does the description of Christ in Part III as "a Baby / new born! / among the words" (P, 263). The view recalls as well the artist-priest imagery of *Dubliners* (1914) and *A Portrait of the Artist as a Young Man* (1916) and may well have derived from James Joyce, whom Williams greatly admired and whose entrance into *Paterson* in terms of *Ulysses* (1922) and *Finnegans Wake* (1939) has been generally acknowledged. One can see, too, how in such a remythologizing of Christianity Williams' search for a "redeeming language" becomes important as an equivalent to the kind of communion normally associated with Christ's birth and sacrifice.

Moreover, to enforce the deliberateness of this secularization of the Word become flesh (John 1 : 14), it is foreshadowed in the secularization of many of his poem's other biblical allusions. In *Paterson I* (1946), "Jacob's ladder" (Genesis 28 : 12) is turned into "a long, rustic, winding stairs in the gorge leading to the opposite side of the river" (P, 26), converting Heaven into a local tavern, and, in the work's Preface, God's being "the beginning and the end" (Revelation 21 : 6) becomes a model for poetic composition. The history of this equation of God and the imagination is at least as old as *Kora,* where the poet had written: "There is neither beginning nor end to the imagination but it delights in its own seasons reversing the usual order at will" (I, 35).

Those critics who would not see these new contexts of the unicorn myth and who would approach Williams' descriptions of the tapestries as examples of a literalism like that suggested by his misunderstanding of Imagism or by the descriptive practices of Louis Agassiz may miss much of what is original in the poem. Although Williams may reverse his doubts about the ability of art to survive, he does not alter his opposition to art as copying. The stress on imitation which his *Autobiography* (1951) indicates he reached about 1923 still applies: "To copy is merely to reflect something already there, inertly. . . . But by imitation we enlarge nature itself, we become nature or we discover in ourselves nature's active part" (A, 241). The doubling of art and life which results from this process and which accounts for some of the confusion in his last books allows for the patterns of descent and return that characterize his continued uses of the Kora myth, the figure of "the wise old man," and the problem of "mean-

155

ing." The wise old man—or Demeter in the Kora legend
—again appears to challenge hopeless and desperate situations and rescue the writer from the inundations of life,
not in any transcendental way but in a way consistent with
Jung's "Archetypes of the Collective Unconscious," as a
vision of the future rescues one from the present or as one
moves from Sartrean nausea to freedom. Art's conversion
of undigested experience into knowledge makes such rescues possible.

Williams expresses this function of art as rescuer in a
number of late works. *I Wanted to Write a Poem* describes the hopeless and desperate situation prompting
"Sub Terra" (1915), and the *Autobiography* details a similar mood for *Kora*. *Paterson III* makes specific its presentation of art as a rescuer of man from inundation: "The
writing / should be a relief, / relief from the conditions /
which as we advance become—a fire, / a destroying fire"
(P, 137). Indeed, the allusion to the Verteuil tapestry
which occurs later in the book comes shortly after a reference to "Persephone [Kora] gone to hell" (P, 151). Williams' *A Dream of Love* has Doc Thurber continue the
notion by showing his need to get away from his practice
one afternoon a week in order to write. In the play,
Thurber goes on to explain that the rescuer need not "be
a woman, but she's the generic type. It's a woman—even
if it's a mathematical formula for relativity. Even more so
in that case—but a woman" (ML, 200). Thurber indicates that it might even be "a poem": "I mean a woman
[poem], bringing her up to the light, building her up and
not merely of stone or colors or silly words—unless he's
supremely able—but in the flesh, warm, agreeable, made
of pure consents" (ML, 200). The description of the

156

woman-poem, which is the Kora myth, echoes the poet's location of the inspiration for art in *Kora* "at the sickening turn toward death," and the art work as "a thing to carry up with you on the next turn" (I, 71). Williams thus carefully fits *Paterson V* into his previous treatments of the Kora pattern and art and makes possible a view of the book not only as a coda of *Paterson I–IV* but also as an extension of "Asphodel, That Greeny Flower." At one time intended to be *Paterson V*, "Asphodel" makes more open use of the Kora legend; in it, Demeter as the image of relativity acts as rescuer in the coda. The final celebration of light by which the movement of all objects is measured drenches the poem's themes—including medieval pageantry, pomp, and ceremony—and forms its moment of truth. Here, pageantry—the process of sacramentalization or dance by which experience is converted into knowledge—becomes more important and, although Williams' cockney grandmother emerges as Demeter, one may assume that the formality of the dance is the final rescuer of man from the subjectivism and "lateral sliding" of sentimental language. At least, Williams uses the seventh tapestry in "A Formal Design" (1959) and is able to resolve the work without recourse to his grandmother, by merely asserting the formality of the tapestry's composition.

Williams employs the same care to integrate "Pictures from Brueghel" with his previous treatments of the painter. For example, he excludes *The Peasant Dance* or *Kermess* (c. 1567) from the sequence and its usual pairing with *Peasant Wedding* and, in "The Adoration of the Kings," he alludes directly to *Paterson V* and "the Nativity / which I have already celebrated." In place of *Kermess,*

which forms the basis of "The Dance" (1942), he uses *The
Wedding Dance in the Open Air* (1566). The reader is
thus encouraged to go to the earlier treatments and their
contexts to supplement his understanding of these later
works. "The Dance" first appeared in *Palisade* magazine
and later in *The Wedge* (1944) between "Paterson: The
Falls" and "Writer's Prologue to a Play in Verse." Its inclusion here suggests early the poet's predisposition to
make Brueghel one strand of *Paterson*. The poem gives
no evidence that Williams knows that a kermesse is a
saint's day. He describes the arrangement of the panel
with no mention of the peasant dressed in the traditional
costume of a fool or the church in the background ignored
by the figures or the picture of the Madonna which looks
down on the revelers from the tree on the right. Nor does
he mention the two children in the foreground imitating
their dancing elders. Williams' concerns are again secular.
He highlights the corpulent dancers, "kicking and rolling
about / the Fair Grounds" to "the squeal and the blare
and the / tweedle of bagpipes, a bugle and fiddles" (CLP,
11). Yet Brueghel's "great picture" contains no bugle and
fiddles, and dancing, particularly to bagpipe music, as
Fritz Grossmann indicates in *The Paintings of Brueghel*,
"appears mostly as something sinful in Brueghel's works." [16]
Grossmann writes that *The Peasant Dance* not only depicts the sin of lust but the figures seated at the table illustrate as well the sins of anger and gluttony. He goes on
to note, "The man next to the bagpipe player wears on his
hat the peacock feather of vain pride." [17] Like many
Brueghel pictures, it seems designed to illustrate a Flemish
proverb; in this instance, "As their elders sing, so pipe
the young folks."

None of the moralizing enters Williams' poem; the poet's main concern at this time becomes his perennial problem of gauging life to measure. In particular, he celebrates the bearing up of Brueghel's sound, swinging butts and shanks to what he imagines by their postures to be rollicking measures, and the image of "swinging weight" returns to complete "Pictures from Brueghel." The very change of the title of the painting to "The Dance" indicates the concern, for "dance," as he is clear to acknowledge in both *Kora* and his essay on *Leaves of Grass,* hinges precisely on an interplay of life and art. The poem's stress on measure suggests that the poet is more susceptible to the view of Brueghel as a master of monumental forms, rhythms, colors, and moving masses and as a transformer of life and the particular into art and the universal than to the image of him as an illustrator of proverbs. This belief, which makes Brueghel a kind of proto-Williams, agrees with views like that expressed in Robert Delevoy's *Bruegel* (1959): "When he broke the long silence of the Gothic epoch and ushered in the art of modern times with depictions of the boisterous rejoicings of the populace, and when he broke with a tradition of religious art, it was because 'he descended from the world of the eternal into the present.' . . . He was not a painter of peasants but a great humanist. . . . And this is why he could be so supreme an interpreter of everyday life and succeeded in creating a style so well adapted to the merrymakings of the populace." [18]

 This is not to suggest that Williams was ignorant of Brueghel's moralizing propensities. The account in *Autobiography* of his meeting with Adrienne Monnier reveals an awareness of Brueghel's symbolism: "Somehow we got

to talking of Brueghel, whose grotesque work she loved—
the fish swallowing a fish that itself was swallowing another. She enjoyed the thought, she said, of pigs scream-
ing as they were being slaughtered, a contempt for the
animal" (A, 193). The passage repeats in almost the same
words an account of the meeting given in *In the American
Grain* (IAG, 106–107). Mrs. Williams, who writes that
the Brueghel poems—"Landscape with the Fall of Icarus,"
"The Hunters in the Snow," and "The Wedding Dance
in the Open Air"—derive from Thomas Craven's *A Treasury of Art Masterpieces, from the Renaissance to the
Present Day* (1939), suggests one possible reason for the
lack of moralizing here. Like Delevoy, Craven tends to
play up the figure of a painter whose broad interests in
people and the whole business of living led him to delve
"into the homely stuff around him" and convert "it into
dramatic art." Craven, who opposes Brueghel's sensibility
to Bosch's "grotesque ideology of the Middle Ages," [19]
makes no mention of the moralistic purpose of the panels,
though his description of Brueghel's recovery of esteem
after three centuries of neglect must have struck sympathy
later when, after *Paterson I*, Williams' own reputation began to solidify. This moralizing purpose is simply to be
ignored for the moment in favor of other characteristics.

Paterson V, detailing *The Adoration of the Kings*
(1564), one of Brueghel's only two upright paintings, continues this neglect of moral purpose. Critics note that it
is the first painting by Brueghel composed almost exclu-
sively of large figures and that its composition is closely
related to Italian art. Yet for Williams these considera-
tions pale before other facts. The composition is made to
echo his interest in what the old leave the young and

center dually on the baby about whom the richly clad kings cluster and the old man surrounded by a ragged soldiery. The baby, through the kings' gifts, assumes the qualities of language rescued by art while the old man takes on many qualities of dwindling life. The groupings represent emblematically the contending forces which the imagination seizes upon to produce the "picture of perfect rest" mentioned in Kora "as the basis of permanence in art" (I, 32–33). The Virgin, who in Brueghel is central to the composition, is completely ignored by Williams' stabilizing forces, and one can understand why. In the emblems which the central figures take up—the greybeard as artist, the baby as language rescued by art—the figure of the Virgin becomes the artistic process. Thus for Williams the Virgin is both the still center of the panel and the whole panel, and by speaking as he does of the entire panel, he is, though not mentioning her, in effect delineating her. Since the original does not emphasize the mysterious, his secularization of the Nativity is not itself out of character, but one might question whether the painter would have approved of the particular meaning that Williams gives his composition, or his identification of the greybeard as the child's father, or the kings' gifts in "The Gift" (1956) as "all that love can bring." One can see from these first appearances of Brueghel that Williams' use of Brueghel as a master whom a writer might imitate without going astray involved on Williams' part a great deal of distortion and self-deception.

The particular inclusion of Brueghel in a section of Paterson given over to tapestries—though perhaps intended as early as the inclusion of "The Dance" in The Wedge—may reflect Williams' awareness of Brueghel's indebtedness to the tapestry cartoon for some of his effects. Early in his career Brueghel is believed to have worked for Pieter Coeck, "a highly esteemed designer of tapestry cartoons." *Time* in 1957 remarked: "The widespread taste for everyday scenes for home decorations was handled in tapestries for the rich; for the less well-to-do, it fell to the 'stayned clothe' works on perishable fine linen turned out by the watercolorists. It was to this tradition, with its set format, sharply delineated forms and flat surfaces, that Brueghel himself turned, developing it in his oils to the level of great art." [20] Delevoy adds, "At most one may perhaps be justified in seeing the influence of the tapestry designer in the markedly vertical structure of Brueghel's earliest large-scale compositions." [21]

Williams' neglect of Brueghel's moralizing tendencies and alterations of Brueghel's panels to suit his own ends continue in the ten poems which form the title sequence of *Pictures from Brueghel*. To emphasize Brueghel's shaping intelligence and what Williams believes is the relationship between an artist and his work, he begins the work with a "Self-Portrait." In the *Hudson Review*, this "Self-Portrait" was kept separate from the rest of the sequence, which began its numbering with "Landscape with the Fall of Icarus." The poem is set in winter, and winter, as often in Williams' work, conveys dwindling life. This suggestion is reinforced by the "old man" image of the artist, recalling the greybeard of *Paterson V;* and, as the infant Christ had there predicted one kind of flowering as art, this figure's "bulbous nose" predicts a second. Unfortunately, the aptness of these chance associations is undermined by the fact that the panel is not by Brueghel. As art historians like R. J. M. Begeer have established, its subject is the Jester Gonnella, who lived in Ferrara at the court of Niccolò III d'Este (1393–1444). Currently the painting is assigned to an anonymous southern follower of Jan van Eyck; but, when Williams visited Vienna in April 1924, it was still being ascribed to Brueghel under the titles *The Shepherd* and *Head of a Peasant*.

A Voyage to Pagany (1928) mentions going to a Brueghel exhibit in Vienna and ending up in the Parliament building and, in *"Paterson:* Listening to Landscape" (1970), Sister Bernetta Quinn relates that Williams while in Vienna greatly loved to visit the Brueghels hanging in the Kunsthistorisches Museum. The original title for the poem, "Self-Portrait: The Old Shepherd," bears this out. But, suppose, as did Williams, that the panel was by Brueghel. Behind the ironies of a painter masked as a shepherd and exposed by virtue of his delicate wrists lie the legends of Carel van Mander's *Schilderboeck* (1604), repeated by *Time* and Delevoy, that Brueghel was a practical joker and that he and Hans Franckert "often went out into the country to see the peasants at their fairs and weddings. Dressed up as peasants, they brought gifts like the other guests, claiming a relationship with the bride or groom." [22] In these legends one can see Williams' own self-image as a playful poet-doctor among the weddings and sufferings of the poor reasserting a close affinity with the painter.

"Landscape with the Fall of Icarus," the second poem of the sequence, is more safely attributable to Brueghel, though there is some question if either of its extant versions was actually executed by the master. Set in spring, when the artist would be liberated by art from winter, the panels constitute Brueghel's sole use of mythological themes. They illustrate the moral of man's trying to exceed his natural limits as well as the Flemish proverb: "No plow stands still just because a man dies." Again Williams takes liberties with his source, for his poem records that the farmer was "sweating in the sun / that melted / the wings' wax" (PB, 4). Yet the panels show the sun low over the horizon, suggesting either dawn or dusk. If dawn, one wonders how there has been enough heat to melt the wings and, if dusk, how high Icarus flew to take so long a fall from his midday hubris. Brueghel wryly undercuts Ovid's description of the blind shepherd and dazed farmer who thought Daedalus and Icarus were gods by having them ignore the drowning youth, and Williams preserves the theme of indifference with words like "concerned with itself," "unsignificantly," and "unnoticed." Sister Bernetta Quinn finds this quality of unmindfulness long before any actual mention of Brueghel is made in *Paterson,* in the vignettes which comprise parts of Book II (1948): "Neither river nor church spire intrudes into the game going on below, a world which the poet can see from his summit, a watchtower somewhat akin to Brueghel's pinnacle." [23] In *William Carlos Williams* (1968), Thomas R. Whitaker sees disjunctive details and values as characteristic of these final poems, and in this light one may read "Landscape" as one reads "Asphodel," with its stream of consciousness technique, as the combined *modus proferendi* and *ars poetica* of Williams' final vision.

Williams moves to "The Hunters in the Snow." The artist and his practice have been introduced and the setting is once more winter—a new facet-plane; a starting over. With this poem one begins to recognize in the clear disregard for the order in which the panels were painted an equally clear reversal of seasons which may well have started with "Icarus" but which extends to the next five segments. Winter is shown moving backward through autumn into summer. In " 'Parody as Initiation': The Sad Education of *Dorian Gray*," Jan B. Gordon finds the same seasonal regress in Oscar Wilde's novel and associates it with the *fin-de-siècle* tendency to die into art. For Williams, whose myth of art is Kora and who in *Kora* had already described the imagination's ability to reverse seasons, the regress is ostensibly life (winter) descending into Hades to reemerge as art (spring). In this case, as in "Asphodel," the usual futurity of the descent is subordinated to a reconciliation with the past. By having to go through the harvests of "Peasant Wedding" and "Haymaking" before hitting high summer, the reader is forced to accept Williams' comment in "The Tortuous Straightness of Charles Henri Ford" (1939) that in a master a fusion must occur between the dreams he dreamed when he was young and the world of his later years. In old age, this fusion can be brought about only by retracing time, much as Williams does by rearranging the panels.

One of an unfinished series of months painted for Niclaes Jonghelinck, *The Hunters in the Snow* (1565) is most famous as pure landscape. Critics cite its lack of symbolic background and its stress on the organic and natural. In Williams' re-creation, where one would expect normally the same secular stress, one detail is exaggerated. He describes the inn-sign as "a stag a crucifix / between his antlers" (PB, 5). The sign shows a stag, true enough, but it also shows a haloed, praying figure. Neither occupies an important place on the panel. To stress this one religious image in a panel so predominantly secular would seem odd except that the crucifix does prepare the reader in an obverse way for the birth of Christ which occurs in the next winter scene, "The Adoration of the Kings." Here, repeating the panel which he treated in *Paterson V,* Williams again tells his reader what to expect. He celebrates "the alert mind dissatisfied with / what it is asked to / and cannot do / accept the story" (PB, 6). Like Brueghel, who breathes new life into a set image, Williams will make changes in his source. These changes will consist in giving new meaning to what is already present as well as providing new details and perspectives.

The "head of ripe wheat" on the wall beside the bride makes the setting of "Peasant Wedding" unmistakably autumn. The dimensions of Brueghel's panel suggest that the painting was a companion to *The Peasant Dance,* already treated by Williams in "The Dance." The painting, which carries over some of the same images as *The Peasant Dance,* is believed to represent gluttony. Critics support this belief by noting details such as the man pouring beer or wine in the foreground, the still-life arrangement of the mugs, the greedy child whose peacock feather again represents vanity, the young man grabbing pies off the makeshift tray, the spoon in the hatband of one server (also in *The Peasant Dance*), the guests at the table drinking and stuffing themselves, and the crush of the crowd outside waiting to be admitted. In *Peter Bruegel, the Elder,* H. Arthur and Mina C. Klein account for these unseated guests by reminding the viewer, "the 'sitdown guests' around the table number about twenty, the maximum permitted for such peasant celebrations by the decrees of Charles V, which were continued in effect by Philip II." [24] Yet no available information seems to

166

aid the critics in determining the identity of either the groom or the bearded guest talking to the friar. One noted Brueghel expert, Gustav Glück, believes the groom is the glutton seated at the table with the spoon in his mouth; Baron von den Elst asserts the groom is not there, that the panel depicts another Flemish proverb: "It's a poor man who is not able to eat at his own wedding." Gilbert Highet ventures that the groom is the man in the store-bought clothes leaning back to ask for more beer, and Williams says it is the man pouring the wine or beer. As for the bearded guest, Williams thinks he is the mayor and others have conjectured he is a landlord or a squire. Williams' re-creation of the panel leaves out entirely the crush of the crowd. He replaces color balance with verbal equivalents, reconstructing the painting about the simple silence of the bride and the gabbing "women in their starched headgear." The awkward posture of the bride recalls the "downcast eyes of the Virgin" in the Nativity poem.

As realized by Williams, "Haymaking" is also set in late summer or early autumn. Rather than the hay which is being harvested in Brueghel's painting, wheat is being cut down. The action recalls the mention of "a head of ripe wheat" in "Peasant Wedding," regressing from bound to uncut grain much in the same way that the crucifix of "The Hunters in the Snow" regresses into the birth of "The Adoration of the Kings" and the downcast virgin-mother of "The Adoration" regresses into the just-married virgin of "Peasant Wedding." The details of the panel are hardly touched on by the poem, which stresses not the panel but the living quality of the man who creates his own magpies and patient horses. The same sense of self-created worlds is carried over to "The Corn Harvest," where a reverse mirror image is offered in the poet's shift from the painter to a "young / reaper enjoying his / noonday rest" (PB, 9). Sleep as well as art has its magpies and patient horses. The poem is, as Franklyn suggests, romantic, a "portrait of the good folk enjoying the simple things." It continues the view of Brueghel set out in van Mander and the sequence's opening poem; it may add, also, memories of the Italian peasants Williams describes in *A Voyage to Pagany:* "Peasants were coming into the fields. There were magpies, a bird he knew, in the young trees, magpies and crows in the furrows" (VP, 95). Williams does overlook the women "stuffing their faces almost like animals over carrion." [25] Likewise, he does overlook the men playing bowls behind the wheatfield in the middle distance of the panel and the panel's split between work and recreation. Williams' young man has already overeaten and unbuttoned his pants and his being in the sunlight focuses, as the "resting center" of their workaday world, a Land of Cockaigne whose dreamy silence in Williams is everywhere attacked as being ineffective (nonaction producing), sentimental, and false. In the shade, women gossip, opposing this silence with the roar of perhaps an empty language.

The Wedding Dance in the Open Air, which replaces *The Peasant Dance* as the companion piece to *Peasant Wedding,* prompts a return to the sense of circling that Williams had used earlier in "The Dance." It, too, takes up with its noise and women in "starched / white headgear" images and echoes from elsewhere in the sequence. Instead of the awkward bride or the sleeping "young reaper," the discipline of the artist is used to oppose their sound. The barn and seated guests of "Peasant Wedding" give way to market square and dancing, and the hunters emerging from "icy mountains" in "The Hunters in the Snow" reform into the figures going "openly towards the wood's edge." As usual in Brueghel, dancing and bagpipe music appear as sinful, and here, critics feel, Brueghel's wedding is a pretext for lust rather than grace. Williams prefers to ignore this moral for the appearance of "a simple genre scene without deeper significance," but the piece, also, by its weight of echoes and its shift toward the control of art, suggests that he is beginning to restate and reinterpret his themes for the sequence's close.

"The Parable of the Blind" continues the suggestion. Words like "red" and "unshaven" bring the reader back to the sequence's opening poem—another beginning; another facet-plane. Like the readers, the beggars are caught in a regressive movement between "peasant cottage" (Poems VIII–V) and "church spire" (Poems IV–III). Their motion is made to parody that proper to an artist and the creative cycle of Kora: they move "diagonally downward / across the canvas" their faces "raised / as toward the light" (PB, 11). Since, as in Matthew (15:14) they lead others "triumphantly to disaster" and by their blindness miss the real light that saturates the end of "Asphodel, That Greeny Flower," they symbolize a kind of false artist. Their situation recalls the poet's earlier damning of the faithless artist in "Against the Weather" (1939). But here "faith" must not be interpreted as traditional Christianity, the Church, or mysticism—all of which Williams shows evidence of rejecting in a 1951 letter to Frank L. Moore. Rather the faith is close to that described by John Ruskin in *Modern Painters* (1855): "The greatest thing a human soul ever does in the world is to *see* something and tell what it *saw* in a plain way. Hundreds of people can talk for one who can think, but thousands can think for one who can see. To see clearly is poetry, prophecy, and religion,—all in one." [26] Williams' Brueghel with "the eyes red-rimmed / from over-use he must have / driven them hard" (PB, 3) illustrates the difficulty of this seeing.

"Children's Games" ends the sequence. A reproduction of the Brueghel panel on which it is based hung prominently in the picture-lined Williams livingroom. Thought to be part of a planned "ages of man" series, the panel depicts adult-looking children absorbed in their games with the seriousness devoted by grownups to their affairs. These children in Williams reverse the image of the old man on which the sequence began and seem to suggest Christ's admonition that "Except ye be converted, and become as little children, ye shall not enter into the kingdom of heaven" (Matthew 18 : 3). They realize the poet's redeeming image of life as a dance and also recall his earlier images of poetry and of the relationship between life and art as dances. The three dances perhaps are meant to combine into the general dance he describes in "Danse Pseudomacabre" (1920): "Everything that varies a hair's breadth from another is an invitation to the dance. Either dance or annihilation. There can be only the dance of ONE" (FD, 210). Nevertheless, this general dance contains images of potential disaster associated with blindness in the blindman's buff of Part II and the attempts "to drag / the other down blindfold" in Part III. Opposed to this blindness is the artist, who continues in his role of seeing man. Not represented in *The Parable of the Blind* (1568) but presenting the parable, Brueghel is celebrated at the poem's close: "Brueghel saw it all / and with his grim / humor faithfully / recorded / it" (PB, 14). The work of art returns to its initial authorial vision.

Despite the presence of all these regressive images in the sequence, a counterdirection channels it through a progressive history of Western thought. This history, which moves from classical times (Poem II) to medieval Christianity (Poems III–IV) to Renaissance secularism (Poems V–VIII) to modern skepticism (Poems IX–X), recalls the several histories of culture from Homer to the Atomic Age that occur in "Asphodel, That Greeny Flower." Much as Brueghel's sixteenth-century figures set the tone of the fall of Icarus and Christ's nativity, this skepticism provoked by man's choosing the momentary over the absolute colors the entire sequence with a Kierkegaardian aestheticism. The aestheticism recalls Matthew Arnold's statement in "The Study of Poetry" (1880) that the betrayal of religion by its materialization in fact would force man to rely increasingly on poetry. Although what Arnold meant by "unconscious poetry" is more like Williams' view of "sentimental language," the various facet-planes into which the individual parts of the sequence fall bear out by their new starts and abrupt shifts Williams' continuing reliance on poetry and art as a major source of wisdom now that one can no longer rely on divinity. His final interpretation of experience in terms of the modern facet-planes of cubism rather than the illusions created by Brueghel's paintings attests to the poem's overriding difference from the original. Here one might argue that the analytic cubism of "Pictures from Brueghel" is a step backward from the synthetic cubism of *Paterson*, but one can see that in writing the sequence Williams offers a perspective compatible with the reworking of the unicorn legend and the secularizing of the Incarnation that marked *Paterson V.*

Thus, by avoiding a premise that the poems of these final volumes may be reliable guidebook transcriptions, a reader may begin to notice the real intention of the liberties which the poet takes and the consequent nature of the poems' originality. What the tapestries and panels represent is not a crutch for what a few critics have hinted is a writer's failing imagination but a principle of exclusion in a poetics which, by having made poetry an extension of personality, had grown to include anything. As Williams says in the Mike Wallace interview of *Paterson V:* "Anything is good material for poetry. Anything" (P 262). Yet, if anything is good material for poetry, the poet must devise a means for knowing what to leave out; what to save for another poem. Sub-personalities must be formed. In *Paterson,* Williams creates Dr. Paterson for this purpose; in these volumes, he revives the weavers and Brueghel. These creations and revivals, moreover, are clearly separate from the epical stances advocated by Joyce and Eliot. Rather than a way of giving order, of bringing contemporary experience rigorously into line with the past, allowing present and past to function as tenor and vehicle of some organizational metaphor along the lines of exact recurrence, Williams subscribes to a principle of distorted returns similar to that which his friend Wallace Stevens advocated, and common to the cyclical returns of Vorticism. All minds distort individually but, keeping with his views of sex and poetry, Williams is interested ultimately in only those minds which manifest their differences in "things." Through the image of the dance, which objectifies these differences in the muscle, Williams avoids the interiorization that produces Stevens' acts of the imagination and Williams' early attack on Stevens in his Prologue to *Kora*. Like the fifteenth-century philosopher, Nicholas of Cusa, Williams denies that intellectual functions can exist dissociated from the realm of sensible material and insists that the act of thought be in harmony with the organization of the body. No two people's eyes have the same vision, but if vision is objectified in action, one may get the sort of continuity that produces medicine and science and by which past and present forms of the state may be judged.

Here Williams' theory and practice most resembles what H. A. Mason's *Humanism and Poetry in the Tudor Court* describes as Sir Thomas Wyatt's use of Petrarch to shape his own views. In discussing "The Piller Perished," Mason proposes that "Wyatt used his originals as a Mask or Persona, as a means of finding and creating himself. His best translations, so far from being proof that he was a derivative poet or an unskilled translator, show that he was an independent critic of his sources."[27] "Wyatt's reason for departing from Petrarch," according to Mason, "was to enable him to handle strong personal feeling for Cromwell."[28] In this manner, Mason supports his premise that "Wyatt's translations are more truly autobiographical than his so-called lyrics."[29] Identical with Mason's arguments are those used in the same year by Williams' friend, Theodore Roethke. In "How to Write Like Somebody Else," he responded to attacks on *Words for the Wind* (1957) that his poetry had become overly derivative from W. B. Yeats by claiming that the very fact a writer "has the support of a tradition, or an older writer, will enable him to be more himself—or more than himself." [30] Moreover, in accepting as vehicles for interpreting experience these masks derived from art works, either his own or others, Williams adds to Arnold's position on poetry a view similar to Wilde's in "The Decay of Lying" (1889) that life imitates art and that, for instance, were it not for art one would not know fogs: "At present, people see fogs, not because there are fogs, but because poets and painters have taught them the mysterious loveliness of such effects. There may have been fogs for centuries in London. I dare say there were. But no one saw them, and so we do not know anything about them. They did not exist till Art had invented them." [31] A sympathy with Wilde's view is also apparent in Williams' recurrent image of the poet as a discoverer whose discovery is then usurped by the herd, forcing him either to become one of the herd or to go on making new discoveries, as James Fenimore Cooper's Natty Bumpo did.

The combination of this aestheticism, Williams' use of mask, and Wilde's view of life as an imitation of art reinforces the image of the artist as voyeur which Williams repeatedly asserts. Much as Penelope in Sir John Davies' Orchestra (1596), by watching others dance, participates in a larger, measured cosmic dance, so too does Williams' voyeuristic poet. From a vantage point outside yet still very much within its procreative effects, he asserts the need for one to join others in the process of dancing, but his assertion makes him, like Brueghel's "shaping intelligence," already part of the dance. This almost neoplatonic view of the dance may derive from Roethke who in 1952 had written of it in "Four for Sir John Davies," but its diagrammatic quality suggests other possible sources in the work of Charles Olson and Robert Duncan. The dance constructs upon the descent-return vertical axis of the Kora pattern a second circle whose horizontal axis ends in love rather than in wisdom and whose image is the dancers. This new circle, Williams' final metaphor for knowledge, becomes his legacy to those young people who would come after him and who in the obtuseness and cruelty and blinding light of young love do not yet have time for art.

The remaining poems of the volume revert to familiar themes and interests. More given to physical detail than were the short poems of *The Desert Music* and *Journey to Love*, they return the reader to life as a source of poetry. Perhaps in echo of the overriding theme of the Brueghel poems, many depict life's crystallization into art. The beauty of roses in "To Flossie" (1957) lies frozen in a refrigerator or equally, as "Poem: The rose fades" (1958) proposes, into art. "He Has Beaten about the Bush Long Enough" (1961) describes intellection freezing into "the crystal- / line pattern / of / new ice on / a country pool" (PB, 29), and the movement is repeated by the drifts into freezing winter characterizing works like "The Woodthrush" (1961), "The Polar Bear" (1961), "Jersey Lyric" (1961), and "To a Woodpecker" (1960). All seem related to the image of Villon's frozen ink pot at the close of his *Petit Testament*, used by Williams as early as "Notes from a Talk on Poetry" (1919) to illustrate how emotion freezes into art. Similarly the "glossy leg" of *Kora in Hell*, whose text had been reissued in 1957 by City Lights Books, recurs in the walking girls of "Perpetuum Mobile" (1959), the calves of "Chloe" (1959), and the woman of "Mounted as an Amazon" (1957). Dance in the senses of both *Kora* and "Children's Games" figures prominently in the several poems written to Williams' grandchildren and in lyrics whose titles suggest dance as their subject. Triadic measures recur in poems like "The Gift" and "The Turtle" (1956), capturing this element of the past for the volume, and other poems like "The Stolen Peonies" (1959) and "The Fruit" (1959) echo "Asphodel" 's return from infidelity. The interplay of sexes underlies many of the works, but specifically those entitled simply "Song."

Critics such as Hugh Kenner are willing to place a poem like "Song: Beauty is a shell" (1960) among Williams' best, most poignant, and loveliest achievements. In "William Carlos Williams: In Memoriam" (1963), he writes: "He had brought the language by concern and love to an utter, feminine responsiveness" (PWCW, 116), and Peter Meinke's "William Carlos Williams: Traditional Rebel" (1967) speaks of "a sort of *revivification by rearrangement* of the rhythms of blank verse" in these late works (PWCW, 108). He cites the inclusion of Spenser's iambics into the structure of "Asphodel" as one instance of it in the long poems, and one does detect a lessening syncopation in the rhythms of many of these later works. The nervousness which added to the jerky movement and the vividness of the early lyrics is now smoothed into something else, and this new smoothness suggests perhaps a too easy facility in the handling of detail. All these lyrics seem shaped to the vision of the larger, less lyrical poems as if they were written not so much as fresh, independent observations but as brief confirmations of these already enunciated systems and visions. At times the largeness of the vision leads even to a disregard for the whatness of objects. In "Heel & Toe to the End" (1961), for instance, Yuri Gagarin's history-making first flight into space is converted into the heel and toe neoplatonic dance of "Children's Games" as if this and not physical reality were its primary consideration. One might even accuse the poet of sliding here into the sentimental language he had earlier attacked. In fact, he accuses himself of it by dismissing the poems as a "going down hill rapidly." He told Stanley Koehler in a *Paris Review* interview that he considered them "too regular." [32]

Certainly, in these final lyrics one senses the problem of sequence for a poet who proposes that his life work turn back upon itself and yet remain expansive and flexible enough so that he and his desires may not wither and die. Like Don Quixote who, in the second half of Cervantes' novel, must live up to a reputation imposed by his early exploits, the poet must as consciously preserve elements vital to his relationship to the past. As the don must repeat the actions which earned him his following, so too must the poet; what seems to be a confirmation in these poems may in reality be self-imitation. Perhaps this is what being a master in the sense advocated by Williams ultimately means and why he finally turns on these late works. Still, it is also true that when accomplished successfully—as Quixote accomplishes the union and as Williams accomplishes it in many of his late, long poems—the fusion by simple variation can provide a reader with unsuspected turns and richnesses. Sections of *Paterson,* "Asphodel, That Greeny Flower," and "Pictures from Brueghel" offer ample proof of this. But such accomplishments, the poet might argue, come from rejecting the spiritual bent of the final chapter of Cervantes' work and from plotting new adventures rather than renewing old themes: the adventures may resemble Quixote's whimsical unrealized plans for an Arcadia, or Huckleberry

Finn's more American lighting out for the territory, or, again, the discoverers' merging with nature in Williams' own *In the American Grain*.

The various "Exercises" suggest an undepicted, virgin world beyond, and Williams' willingness to investigate it continues the belief that "a new world is only a new mind." "Poem: The plastic surgeon" (1962) inaugurates the handling of this new technology, and "Some Simple Measures in the American Idiom and the Variable Foot" (1959) and "Calypso" (1956–1957) willingly engage in new rhythmic experiments. Moreover, the notes which comprise the proposed and unfinished *Paterson VI* suggest that despite all dogmatic pronouncements, there can be no final conclusions. The poet who began his career with an imagined abduction by his grandmother and a baptism into the filthy Passaic ends it fittingly with another echo of this hard-drinking woman in "Mrs. Carmody / an Irish woman / who could tell a story / when she'd a bit taken" (P, 284). Williams as a poet could not shut his senses off from the changing world about him any more than he could as a doctor, and so long as he could immerse himself in that new world his writing remained inventive, vital, and productive. Wallace Stevens thus characterized him in a letter to José Rodríguez Feo (1953), "He is a man who is interested in anything new that may be going around, the chances are that he has interested himself in the subject and I suppose that the only way to interest yourself in such a subject is to associate with [it]." [33] Earlier he had written Williams about this characteristic, "One never detects paraphrase in anything you do, either personally or in your writing, so that there really is a live contact there." [34] In imitation of that ever expanding universe that he sought to get into his writing and in echo of that insatiable self-fulfilling appetite he described to Riordan in 1926, there could be for Williams only the circle, ever enlarging to encompass more and ever turning upon itself when it had done so: "As I exist, omnivorous, everything I touch seems incomplete until I can swallow, digest and make it a part of myself." [35] This is the "lesson" of the later poems.

References

꩜ *Chapter One:* The Man and the Dream

1. Randall Jarrell as quoted on the back cover of *The Sixties,* no. 5 (1961).
2. William Carlos Williams, "In Praise of Marriage," *Quarterly Review of Literature,* II (1945), 147.
3. Ernst Cassirer, *The Individual and the Cosmos in Renaissance Philosophy,* tr. Mario Domandi (Harper Torchbooks, 1963), p. 130.
4. William James, *Pragmatism and Other Essays* (Washington Square Press paperback, 1963), p. 26.
5. Ibid., p. 25.
6. Dora Marsden, "Lingual Psychology," *Egoist,* III (July 1916), 101.
7. William Carlos Williams, "The Great Sex Spiral," *Egoist,* IV (Aug. 1917), 110.
8. John Malcolm Brinnin, *William Carlos Williams* (Minneapolis, 1963), p. 16.
9. William Carlos Williams, "The Editors Meet William Carlos Williams," *A.D. 1952,* III (Winter 1952), 13.
10. Harvey Breit, "Talk with W. C. Williams," *New York Times Book Review* (Jan. 15, 1950), p. 18.

11. William Carlos Williams, "Seventy Years Deep," *Holiday*, XVI (Nov. 1954), 55.

12. William Carlos Williams, "Notes from a Talk on Poetry," *Poetry*, XIV (1919), 214–215, passim.

13. "Seventy Years Deep," p. 55.

14. Ibid.

15. R. P. Blackmur, *Language as Gesture* (New York, 1952), p. 349.

16. Randall Jarrell, Introduction to *Selected Poems of William Carlos Williams* (New York, 1949), p. xv.

17. Carl Jung, *Psyche and Symbol*, ed. Violet S. de Laszlo (Anchor Books, 1952), pp. 70–71.

18. Ibid., pp. 72–73.

19. Ibid., p. 74.

20. Ibid.

21. "Seventy Years Deep," p. 78.

22. William Carlos Williams, "Painting in the American Grain," *Art News*, LIII (June–Aug. 1954), 62, 78.

23. William Carlos Williams, "The Three Letters," *Contact*, III (1921), 10.

24. Joseph N. Riddel, *Modern Language Journal*, LII (1968), 46.

25. William Carlos Williams, "America, Whitman, and the Art of Poetry," *Poetry Journal*, VIII (Nov. 1917), 28–29, passim.

26. "Seventy Years Deep," p. 55.

27. Walter Sutton, "A Visit with William Carlos Williams," *Minnesota Review*, I (1961), 321–322.

28. James, p. 73.

29. Sutton, "Visit," p. 322.

30. Charles P. Steinmetz, *Four Lectures on Relativity and Space* (New York, 1923), p. 7.

31. A. N. Whitehead, *Science and the Modern World* (Mentor Books, 1948), p. 85.

32. Ibid., pp. 84–85.

33. Steinmetz, p. 121.

34. William Carlos Williams, Introduction to *Transfigured Night* by Byron Vazakas (New York, 1946), p. xiv.

35. Ibid., pp. xii–xiii.

꙰ *Chapter Two: Paterson:* The Dream Extended

1. Wylie Sypher, *Rococo to Cubism in Art and Literature* (Vintage Books, 1960), p. 270.

2. Clement Greenberg, *Art and Culture* (Beacon Books, 1965), p. 71.

3. Ibid., pp. 71–72.

4. Bram Dijkstra, *The Hieroglyphics of a New Speech* (Princeton, 1969), pp. 68–69.

5. Ibid., p. 69.

6. Ibid., p. 72.

7. Ibid., pp. 72–73.

8. H. H. Aranson, *Stuart Davis Memorial Exhibition* (Washington, 1965), p. 17.

9. Stuart Davis as quoted in James Johnson Sweeney, *Stuart Davis* (New York, 1945), p. 10.

10. Gustav Vriesen, "Robert Delaunay's Life and Work from the Beginning to Orphism," in *Robert Delaunay*, by Gustav Vriesen and Max Ihmdahl (New York, 1969), p. 44.

11. Max Ihmdahl, "Delaunay's Position in History," in *Robert Delaunay*, pp. 79–80.

12. Robert Delaunay as quoted in Vriesen, pp. 44, 46.

13. Stuart Davis as quoted in Sweeney, p. 10.

14. Greenberg, p. 75.

15. Ibid., p. 79.

16. Ibid.

17. E. C. Goossen, *Stuart Davis* (New York, 1959), p. 17.

18. Daniel-Henry Kahnweiler, *Juan Gris, His Life and His Work*, tr. Douglas Cooper (New York, 1969), p. 125.

19. As cited by Sister Bernetta Quinn's *"Paterson:* Listening

to Landscape," in *Modern American Poetry*, ed. Jerome Mazzaro (New York, 1970), p. 124.

20. Dijkstra, p. 174.

21. Kahnweiler, p. 141.

22. Quoted in Kahnweiler, p. 193.

23. "On the Possibility of Painting," in Kahnweiler, p. 200.

24. Kahnweiler, pp. 126, 211.

25. Ralph Nash, "The Use of Prose in *Paterson*," *Perspective*, VI (1953), 193–194.

26. Ibid., pp. 196–197.

27. Goossen, p. 18.

28. Ibid., pp. 27–28.

29. Randall Jarrell, *Poetry and the Age* (Vintage Books, 1955), pp. 238–239.

30. Greenberg, p. 154.

31. T. S. Eliot, *Selected Essays* (London, 1951), p. 203.

32. Walter Sutton, "Dr. Williams' *Paterson* and the Quest for Form," *Criticism*, II (1960), 245.

33. Greenberg, p. 155.

34. Jarrell, p. 206.

35. Thomas R. Whitaker, *William Carlos Williams* (New York, 1968), p. 132.

36. Greenberg, p. 157.

37. Sherman Paul, *The Music of Survival* (Urbana, 1968), p. 38.

38. William Carlos Williams, "Letter to an Australian Editor," *Briarcliff Quarterly*, III (Oct. 1946), 208.

39. Richard Gustafson, "William Carlos Williams' *Paterson*," *College English*, XXVI (1964–65), 532.

40. Quinn, p. 129.

41. Quoted by John C. Thirlwall in "William Carlos Williams' *Paterson*," *New Directions 17* (New York, 1961), p. 254.

1. William Carlos Williams, "Poet's Corner," *New Republic,* XCIII (1937), 50.
2. William Carlos Williams, "Seventy Years Deep," *Holiday,* XVI (Nov. 1954), 78.
3. Bram Dijkstra, *The Hieroglyphics of a New Speech* (Princeton, 1969), p. 168.
4. Neil Myers, "William Carlos Williams' *Spring and All,*" *Modern Language Quarterly,* XXVI (1965), 290.
5. James E. Breslin, *William Carlos Williams* (New York, 1950), pp. 55–56.
6. Alan Ostrom, *The Poetic World of William Carlos Williams* (Carbondale, 1966), pp. 20–21.
7. Matthew Arnold, "The Study of Poetry," in *Modern Criticism: Theory and Practice,* ed. Walter Sutton and Richard Foster (New York, 1963), p. 94.
8. W. D. Snodgrass, "Master's in the Verse Patch Again," in *The Contemporary Poet as Artist and Critic,* ed. Anthony Ostroff (Boston, 1964), p. 114.
9. Ibid., p. 115.
10. William Carlos Williams, "Prose about Love," *Little Review,* V (June 1918), 8–9.
11. W. H. Auden as quoted on the back cover of *Pictures from Brueghel* (New York, 1962).
12. J. Hillis Miller, *Poets of Reality* (Cambridge, Mass., 1965), p. 356.
13. Walter Sutton, "A Visit with William Carlos Williams," *Minnesota Review,* I (1961), 315.
14. William Carlos Williams, "Wallace Stevens," *Poetry,* LXXXVII (1956), 238.
15. *New York Times* (April 16, 1953), p. 1.
16. *Life,* XXXIV (May 25, 1953), 38.
17. *Time,* LXI (April 27, 1953), 42.

18. Martin P. Nilsson, *The Mycenaean Origin of Greek Mythology* (Norton Books, 1963), p. 75.

19. Marsden Hartley, *Adventures in the Arts* (New York, 1921), p. 13.

20. William Carlos Williams, "Vs.," *Touchstone,* I (Jan. 1948), 4.

21. Joseph Conrad, *Typhoon and Other Tales* (Signet Books, 1962), p. 222.

꩜ *Chapter Four:* Sex and the Williams Poem

1. William Carlos Williams, "Letter to an Australian Editor," *Briarcliff Quarterly,* III (1946), 205.

2. Ibid., p. 207.

3. Ibid., p. 208.

4. William Carlos Williams, "The Fatal Blunder," *Quarterly Review of Literature,* II (1945), 125–126.

5. Remy de Gourmont, *The Natural Philosophy of Love,* tr. Ezra Pound (New York, 1942), p. 293.

6. Ezra Pound, Translator's Postscript to *The Natural Philosophy of Love,* p. 295.

7. Ibid., pp. 310–311.

8. William Carlos Williams, "The Great Sex Spiral," *Egoist,* IV (Aug. 1917), 111.

9. Otto Weininger, *Sex and Character* (New York, 1908), p. 189.

10. Carl Jung, *Psyche and Symbol,* ed. Violet S. de Laszlo (Anchor Books, 1958), p. 11.

11. Ibid., p. 15.

12. William Carlos Williams, "America, Whitman, and the Art of Poetry," *Poetry Journal,* VIII (Nov. 1917), 27.

13. William Carlos Williams, "Raquel Helene Rose," *Twice-a-Year,* nos. 5–6 (1941), p. 409.

14. Quoted by I. A. Richards in *The Language of Poetry,* ed. Allen Tate (Princeton, 1942), p. 66.

15. Richards, "The Interaction of Words," p. 73.

16. William Carlos Williams, "Robert Lowell's Verse Translation into the American Idiom," *Harvard Advocate*, CXLV (Dec. 1961), 12.

17. Stanley Koehler, "William Carlos Williams," *Writers at Work*, 3d series (New York, 1967), p. 10.

18. *Poetry Journal*, p. 31.

19. William Carlos Williams, "Men . . . Have No Tenderness," *New Directions 7* (New York, 1942), p. 430.

20. Ibid., p. 432.

21. Ibid., p. 436.

22. As quoted in W. D. Snodgrass, "A Rocking Horse: The Symbol, the Pattern, the Way to Live," *Hudson Review*, XI (1958), 197–198.

23. William Carlos Williams, "The Three Letters," *Contact*, III (1921), 12.

24. Quoted in Mike Weaver, *William Carlos Williams: The American Background* (London, 1971), p. 159n.

25. William Carlos Williams, "In Praise of Marriage," *Quarterly Review of Literature*, II (1945), 146–147.

26. Ezra Pound as quoted in Clark Emery's *Ideas into Action* (Coral Gables, 1958), p. 1.

27. "In Praise of Marriage," p. 148.

28. William Carlos Williams, "A Good Doctor's Story," *Nation*, CXLV (1937), 268.

29. Randall Jarrell, *Poetry and the Age* (Vintage Books, 1955), p. 238.

30. William Carlos Williams, "The American Idiom," *Fresco*, I (1960), 15.

31. Walter Sutton, "A Visit with William Carlos Williams," *Minnesota Review*, I (1961), 313.

32. William Carlos Williams, "Sermon with a Camera," *New Republic*, XCVI (1938), 282–283.

33. William Carlos Williams, "Image and Purpose," *New Masses*, XXVIII (Aug. 16, 1938), 26.

34. Ezra Pound, *The Literary Essays of Ezra Pound*, ed. T. S. Eliot (Norfolk, Conn., 1954), p. 21.

35. Carl Jung, *Symbols of Transformation*, tr. R. F. C. Hull (New York, 1956), p. 28.

36. Sutton, p. 323.

37. *Poetry Journal*, p. 28.

ꙮ *Chapter Five:* Brueghel: Descent Once More

1. Denise Levertov, "William Carlos Williams," *Nation*, CXCVI (1963), 230.

2. Ralph Waldo Emerson, "Self-Reliance," in *Ralph Waldo Emerson*, ed. Frederic I. Carpenter (New York, 1934), p. 96.

3. Søren Kierkegaard, *Either/Or*, tr. Walter Lowrie (Princeton, 1949), II, 141.

4. William James, *Pragmatism and Other Essays* (Washington Square Press paperback, 1963), p. 26.

5. Quoted in Mike Weaver, *William Carlos Williams: The American Background* (London, 1971), p. 164.

6. Ralph Nash, "The Use of Prose in *Paterson*," *Perspective*, VI (1953), 194.

7. Jean-Paul Sartre, *Literature and Existentialism*, tr. Bernard Frechtman (New York, 1962), p. 32.

8. Marianne Moore, *Trial Balances*, ed. Ann Winslow (New York, 1935), p. 83.

9. Charles Olson, "*Paterson (Book V)*," *Evergreen Review*, II (Summer 1959), 220.

10. A. Frederick Franklyn, "The Truth and The Poem," *Trace*, no. 48 (May 1963), p. 81.

11. Bram Dijkstra, *The Hieroglyphics of a New Speech* (Princeton, 1969), p. 62.

12. James J. Rorimer, *The Unicorn Tapestries at The Cloisters* (Greenwich, Conn., 1962), pp. 5–6.

13. Ibid., p. 8.

14. Ibid., p. 25.

15. Carl Jung, *Psychology and Alchemy*, tr. R. F. C. Hull (New York, 1952), pp. 450–451.

16. F. Grossmann, *The Paintings of Brueghel* (2d ed.; London, 1966), p. 200.

17. Ibid., p. 202.

18. Robert L. Delevoy, *Bruegel*, tr. Stuart Gilbert (New York, 1959), p. 67.

19. Thomas Craven, *A Treasury of Art Masterpieces, from the Renaissance to the Present Day* (New York, 1939), p. 218

20. *Time*, LXX (Dec. 3, 1957), 65.

21. Delevoy, pp. 14–15.

22. Ibid., p. 23.

23. Sister Bernetta Quinn, *Modern American Poetry,* ed. Jerome Mazzaro (New York, 1970), p. 131.

24. H. Arthur and Mina C. Klein, *Peter Brueghel, the Elder* (New York, 1968), p. 144.

25. Franklyn, pp. 81–82.

26. John Ruskin, *Modern Painters* (Boston, 1900), III, 330–331.

27. H. A. Mason, *Humanism and Poetry in the Early Tudor Court* (London, 1959), pp. 185–186.

28. Ibid., p. 198.

29. Ibid., p. 197.

30. Theodore Roethke, *On the Poet and His Craft,* ed. Ralph J. Mills, Jr. (Seattle, 1969), p. 69.

31. Oscar Wilde, *The Artist as Critic,* ed. Richard Ellmann (New York, 1969), p. 24.

32. Stanley Koehler, "William Carlos Williams," *Writers at Work,* 3rd series (New York, 1967), p. 28.

33. Wallace Stevens, *Letters,* ed. Holly Stevens (New York, 1966), p. 768.

34. Ibid., pp. 245–246.

35. Weaver, p. 164.

Bibliography

꙳

Aranson, H. H. *Stuart Davis Memorial Exhibition.* Washington, D.C., 1965.

Arnold, Matthew. "The Study of Poetry," in *Modern Criticism: Theory and Practice,* ed. Walter Sutton and Richard Foster. New York, 1963.

Blackmur, R. P. *Language as Gesture.* New York, 1952.

Breit, Harvey. "Talk with W. C. Williams," *New York Times Book Review* (Jan. 15, 1950), p. 18.

Breslin, James E. *William Carlos Williams.* New York, 1970.

Brinnin, John Malcolm. *William Carlos Williams.* Minneapolis, 1963.

Cassirer, Ernst. *The Individual and the Cosmos in Renaissance Philosophy,* tr. Mario Domandi. Harper Torchbooks, 1963.

Conarroe, Joel. *William Carlos Williams' 'Paterson': Language and Landscape.* Philadelphia, 1970.

Conrad, Joseph. *Typhoon and Other Tales.* Signet Books, 1962.

Craven, Thomas. *A Treasury of Art Masterpieces, from the Renaissance to the Present Day.* New York, 1939.

Delevoy, Robert L. *Bruegel,* tr. Stuart Gilbert. New York, 1959.

Dijkstra, Bram. *The Hieroglyphics of a New Speech.* Princeton, 1969.

Doyle, Charles. "A Reading of *Paterson III,*" *Modern Poetry Studies,* I (1970), 141–153.

Eliot, T. S. *Selected Essays.* London, 1951.

Ellmann, Richard. *Eminent Domain.* New York, 1967.

Emerson, Ralph Waldo. *Ralph Waldo Emerson,* ed. Frederic I. Carpenter. New York, 1934.

Franklyn, A. Frederick. "The Truth and The Poem," *Trace,* no. 48 (May 1963), 32, 78–83.

Goossen, E. C. *Stuart Davis.* New York, 1959.

Gordon, Jan B. " 'Parody as Initiation': The Sad Education of 'Dorian Gray,' " *Criticism,* IX (1967), 355–371.

Gourmont, Remy de. *The Natural Philosophy of Love,* tr. Ezra Pound. New York, 1942.

Graves, Robert. *The Common Asphodel.* London, 1949.

Greenberg, Clement. *Art and Culture.* Beacon Books, 1965.

Grossmann, F. *The Paintings of Brueghel.* 2d ed. London, 1966.

Gustafson, Richard. "William Carlos Williams' *Paterson,*" *College English,* XXVI (1964–65), 532–534, 539.

Hartley, Marsden. *Adventures in the Arts.* New York, 1921.

Hindus, Milton, ed. *Leaves of Grass One Hundred Years After.* Stanford, 1955.

James, William. *Pragmatism and Other Essays.* Washington Square Press paperback, 1963.

Jarrell, Randall. *Poetry and the Age.* Vintage Books, 1955.

Jung, Carl. *Psyche and Symbol,* ed. Violet S. de Laszlo. Anchor Books, 1952.

——. *Psychology and Alchemy,* tr. R. F. C. Hull. New York, 1952.

——. *Symbols of Transformation,* tr. R. F. C. Hull. New York, 1956.

Kahnweiler, Daniel-Henry. *Juan Gris, His Life and His Work,* tr. Douglas Cooper. New York, 1969.

Kierkegaard, Søren. *Either/Or,* tr. Walter Lowrie. Princeton, 1949. 2 vols.

Klein, H. Arthur, and Mina C. Klein. *Peter Brueghel, the Elder.* New York, 1968.

Koehler, Stanley. "William Carlos Williams," in *Writers at Work.* 3d series. New York, 1967.

Laing, R. D. *The Divided Self.* London, 1960.

Lemaître, Georges. *From Cubism to Surrealism in French Literature.* Cambridge, Mass., 1947.

Levertov, Denise. "William Carlos Williams," *Nation,* CXCVI (1963), 230.

Lowell, Robert. "Paterson II," *Nation,* CLXVI (1948), 692–694.

Marsden, Dora. "Lingual Psychology," *Egoist,* III (July 1916), 95–102.

Mason, H. A. *Humanism and Poetry in the Early Tudor Court.* London, 1959.

Mazzaro, Jerome, ed. *Profile of William Carlos Williams.* Columbus, 1971.

Miller, J. Hillis. *Poets of Reality.* Cambridge, Mass., 1965.

———, ed. *William Carlos Williams.* Englewood Cliffs, 1966.

Myers, Neil. "William Carlos Williams' *Spring and All,*" *Modern Language Quarterly,* XXVI (1965), 285–301.

Nash, Ralph. "The Use of Prose in *Paterson,*" *Perspective,* VI (1953), 191–199.

Nilsson, Martin P. *The Mycenaean Origin of Greek Mythology.* Norton Books, 1963.

Olson, Charles. "*Paterson (Book Five),*" *Evergreen Review,* II (Summer 1959), 220–221.

Ostrom, Alan. *The Poetic World of William Carlos Williams.* Carbondale, 1966.

Paul, Sherman. *The Music of Survival.* Urbana, 1968.

Peterson, Walter Scott. *An Approach to 'Paterson.'* New Haven, 1967.

Pound, Ezra. *The Literary Essays,* ed. T. S. Eliot. Norfolk, Conn., 1954.

Quinn, Sister Bernetta. *"Paterson:* Listening to Landscape," in *Modern American Poetry: Essays in Criticism,* ed. Jerome Mazzaro. New York, 1970.

Richards, I. A. "The Interaction of Words," in *The Language of Poetry,* ed. Allen Tate. Princeton, 1942.

Riddel, Joseph N. "Review of J. Hillis Miller's *William Carlos Williams,"* *Modern Language Journal,* LII (1968), 44–46.

——. "The Wanderer and the Dance: William Carlos Williams' Early Poetics," in *The Shaken Realist: Essays in Modern Literature in Honor of Frederick Hoffman,* ed. M. J. Friedman and John B. Vickery. Baton Rouge, 1970.

Roethke, Theodore. *On the Poet and His Craft,* ed. Ralph J. Mills, Jr. Seattle, 1969.

Rorimer, James J. *The Unicorn Tapestries at The Cloisters.* Greenwich, Conn., 1962.

Ruskin, John. *Modern Painters.* Boston, 1900. 6 vols.

Sartre, Jean-Paul. *Literature and Existentialism,* tr. Bernard Frechtman. New York, 1962.

Snodgrass, W. D. "Master's in the Verse Patch Again," in *The Contemporary Poet as Artist and Critic,* ed. Anthony Ostroff. Boston, 1964.

Steinmetz, Charles P. *Four Lectures on Relativity and Space.* New York, 1923.

Stevens, Wallace. *Letters,* ed. Holly Stevens. New York, 1966.

Sutton, Walter. "Dr. Williams' *Paterson* and the Quest for Form," *Criticism,* II (1960), 242–259.

——. "A Visit with William Carlos Williams," *Minnesota Review,* I (1961), 309–324.

Sweeney, James Johnson. *Stuart Davis.* New York, 1945.

Sypher, Wylie. *Rococo to Cubism in Art and Literature.* Vintage Books, 1960.

Thirlwall, John C. "Ten Years of a New Rhythm," in *Pictures from Brueghel,* by William Carlos Williams. New York, 1962.

——. "William Carlos Williams' *Paterson,"* *New Directions 17.* New York, 1961.

Tyler, Parker. "The Poet of *Paterson Book One,*" *Briarcliff Quarterly*, III (Oct. 1946), 168–175.

Vriesen, Gustav and Max Ihmdahl. *Robert Delaunay.* New York, 1969.

Weaver, Mike. *William Carlos Williams: The American Background.* London, 1971.

Weininger, Otto. *Sex and Character.* New York, 1908.

Whitaker, Thomas R. *William Carlos Williams.* New York, 1968.

Whitehead, A. N. *Science and the Modern World.* Mentor Books, 1948.

Wilde, Oscar. *The Artist as Critic,* ed. Richard Ellmann. New York, 1969.

Williams, William Carlos. *Autobiography.* New York, 1967.

——. *The Collected Earlier Poems.* New York, 1951.

——. *The Collected Later Poems.* New York, 1963.

——. *The Farmers' Daughters.* New York, 1961.

——. *Imaginations.* New York, 1970.

——. *In the American Grain.* New York, 1956.

——. *In the Money.* New York, 1967.

——. *I Wanted to Write a Poem,* ed. Edith Heal. Boston, 1958.

——. *Many Loves.* New York, 1965.

——. *Paterson.* New York, 1963.

——. *Pictures from Brueghel.* New York, 1962.

——. *Selected Essays.* New York, 1954.

——. *Selected Letters.* New York, 1957.

——. *Selected Poems.* New York, 1963.

——. *A Voyage to Pagany.* New York, 1970.

——. *White Mule.* New York, 1967.

——. *Yes, Mrs. Williams.* New York, 1959.

——. "America, Whitman, and the Art of Poetry," *Poetry Journal,* VIII (Nov. 1917), 27–36.

——. "The American Idiom," *Fresco,* I (1960), 15–16.

——. "The Editors Meet William Carlos Williams," *A.D. 1952,* III (Winter 1952), 5–14.

Williams, William Carlos. "The Fatal Blunder," *Quarterly Review of Literature,* II (1945), 125–126.

——. "A Good Doctor's Story," *Nation,* CXLV (1937), 268.

——. "The Great Sex Spiral," *Egoist,* IV (Aug. 1917), 110–111.

——. "Image and Purpose," *New Masses,* XXVIII (Aug. 16, 1938), 23–25.

——. "In Praise of Marriage," *Quarterly Review of Literature,* II (1945), 145–149.

——. "Introduction," *Transfigured Night* by Byron Vazakas. New York, 1946. Pp. ix–xiv.

——. "Letter to an Australian Editor," *Briarcliff Quarterly,* III (Oct. 1946), 205–208.

——. "Men . . . Have No Tenderness," *New Directions 7.* New York, 1942.

——. "Notes from a Talk on Poetry," *Poetry,* XIV (1919), 211–216.

——. "Painting in the American Grain," *Art News,* LIII (June–Aug. 1954), 20–23, 62, 78.

——. "Poet's Corner," *New Republic,* XCIII (1937), 50.

——. "Prose about Love," *Little Review,* V (June 1918), 5–10.

——. "Raquel Helene Rose," *Twice-a-Year,* nos. 5–6 (1941), 402–412.

——. "Robert Lowell's Verse Translation into the American Idiom," *Harvard Advocate,* CXLV (Dec. 1961), 12.

——. "Sermon with a Camera," *New Republic,* XCVI (1938), 282–283.

——. "Seventy Years Deep," *Holiday,* XVI (Nov. 1954), 54–55, 78.

——. "The Three Letters," *Contact,* III (1921), 10–13.

——. "Vs.," *Touchstone,* I (Jan. 1948), 2–7.

——. "Wallace Stevens," *Poetry,* LXXXVII (1956), 234–239.

Winslow, Ann, ed. *Trial Balances.* New York, 1935.

Index

❧

William Carlos Williams

Designed by R. E. Rosenbaum.
Composed by Vail-Ballou Press, Inc.,
in 11 point linotype Baskerville, 2 points leaded,
with display lines in monotype Baskerville.
Printed letterpress from type by Vail-Ballou Press
on Warren's No. 66 text, 60 pound basis,
with the Cornell University Press watermark.
Bound by Vail-Ballou Press
in Columbia book cloth
and stamped in All Purpose foil.

Library of Congress Cataloging in Publication Data
(For library cataloging purposes only)

Mazzaro, Jerome.
  William Carlos Williams: the later poems.

  Bibliography: p.
  1. Williams, William Carlos, 1883–1963. I. Title.
PS3545.I544Z64   811'.5'2   72-11549
ISBN 0-8014-0753-2